LOFT STYLE

LOFT STYLE

Styling your city-center home

Dominic Bradbury

Photographs by Mark Luscombe-Whyte

Watson-Guptill Publications
New York

Text © Dominic Bradbury 2000
Photographs © Mark Luscombe-Whyte 2000
except pages 64, 72(r), 73, 75, 77, 92, 99(r), 100 Elizabeth Whiting Associates;
pages 72(l), 76, 141(r), 167(r) The Interior Archive

First published in the United States in 2001 by Watson-Guptill Publications
a division of BPI Communications, Inc.
770 Broadway, New York, NY 10003
www.watsonguptill.com

Library of Congress Catalog Card Number: 00-105881

ISBN: 0-8230-2840-2

First published in the United Kingdom in 2000
by HarperCollins*Illustrated*
an imprint of HarperCollins*Publishers*
77-85 Fulham Palace Road
London W6 8JB
The HarperCollins Web site address is:
www.**fire**and**water.**com

Color reproduction by Colourscan
Design: Kathryn Gammon
Printed in China

First printing, 2001
1 2 3 4 5 6 7 8 9 / 08 07 06 05 04 03 02 01

ACKNOWLEDGMENTS

Dominic Bradbury and Mark
Luscombe-Whyte would like to
express their gratitude to the following
architects, designers and home
owners who helped to make this book
possible. Thank you for unveiling your
urban spaces.

Architects
Ron Arad & Geoff Crowther, Arc,
Nicholas Burwell, Jamie Falla &
MooArc, Alex Michaelis, Gunnar
Orefelt, David Spence.

Designers
Charles Bateson, Christian de Falbe,
Sophie Douglas, Maria Duff, Christina
Fallah, Malin Iovino, Corin Mellor,
Michael Nathenson, John Roberts,
Steven Roxburghe, Charles Tyler.

Home Owners
Chris Bodker, Eran Ben-Zour, Kurt
Bredenbeck, Gay Longworth & Adam
Spiegel, Anna Norman, Haakon
Overli, Nina Richards, Mark & Claire
Ticktum, Fiona Wase.

And special thanks to Fiona Screen
and Faith Bradbury.

C

ontents

he loft look

Space and light are luxuries in the city. With every square foot and meter at a premium, urban living has become more and more about making the most of all available room, about combining modern utility with a sophisticated, airy look for the home. City living means fighting against claustrophobia in every possible way, opening up living spaces to natural light and promoting a sense of easy freedom and comfort mixed with a designer ethos of contemporary style.

This growing trend towards open living has come to define our times. Little wonder that this trend so often translates into loft living and the transformation of former industrial and commercial buildings — office blocks and schools, factories, warehouses and hospitals — into spacious new apartments. It is these old utilitarian, metropolitan buildings that offer the most obvious opportunities for open-plan living and maximizing sunlight, with their large banks of windows, high ceilings and great unpartitioned spaces.

The powerful and international growth of the loft look in all of its many incarnations has also prompted a reassessment of city living right across the board. Now many apartments and period houses are also being opened up and reconfigured, with the aim of creating larger and more indulgent living spaces, as well as increasing the flow of sunlight right through the home from front to back.

Partition walls are coming down in brownstone terraced houses and nineteenth-century apartment blocks. Skylights are being added, windows enlarged, and glass is being used for doors and partitions — even for walls and floors — all adding to the sense of wellbeing. At the same time, new-build houses across the urban landscape are veering away from traditional, compact multi-room layouts to a more open-plan and informal approach, better suited to our fast-changing lifestyles.

With this wholesale emphasis on open space, on light and the realization of a new design vocabulary in materials and technology for the home, we are adopting and adapting many of the lessons of the pioneering architects of the Modernist era. It was the Modernist godfathers, such as Le Corbusier and Frank Lloyd Wright, who really began to challenge the conventional ways of living, where each room had its own distinct and formalized role. The Modernists began to design homes that prioritized light and open living, making the most of new innovations in glass, steel and artificial lighting to create a new aesthetic.

The houses they created in the 1920s and 30s — Le Corbusier's Villa Savoye in Poissy, France; Frank Lloyd Wright's Falling Water in Bear Run, Pennsylvania; Eileen Gray's E-1027 Seaside House in Roquebrune, France — eventually became design icons. They were ground breaking, innovative, a dramatic architectural response to

◁ **Open-plan living has made this apartment airy and light, despite being situated in a basement space.**

writer Ezra Pound's great rallying call to "make it new." But the spatial lessons of the Modernist pioneers took a long time to filter into the mainstream and make an impact upon the everyday home.

It was only with the start of the loft-living revolution in the 1950s that we really began to under-
stand and appreciate how many of the more liberal principles of the Modernists could best be applied
in a practical sense upon the fabric of the home. Lofts were, in a way, a perfect canvas for the
Modernists and their disciples to play with, yet while the Modernists were busy earning acceptance into
the design establishment, the loft revolution was quietly getting off the ground without them — as a subversive enterprise.

In the 1950s Manhattan artists and bohemians looking for cheap spaces in which to live and work
began to move into old industrial buildings, late-nineteenth- and turn-of-the-century iron-framed buildings that once housed garment sweatshops, laundry companies, furniture and printing workshops, as
well as warehouses and depositories. As industry moved away from Manhattan Island to gain access to
cheaper and larger buildings across the water, the buildings fell empty. Seeing the opportunity to create
a new American version of a Parisian artist's atelier, and lured by the reduced rental bills, painters and
photographers began to move into these spaces not just to work, but to live, and unthinkingly invented
the loft apartment.

The cast-iron frames of these buildings meant that most of the walls were seldom load bearing,
which allowed great sheets of floor-to-ceiling windows and open workshop-style floor plans. They were perfect
studios and galleries for the likes of Robert Rauschenberg, Jasper Johns, Yoko Ono and Willem de Kooning.

The early loft residents of SoHo, and to a lesser extent Greenwich Village, also found these buildings made
fine but basic homes. There was plenty of space and light, while simple partitions to shroud bedrooms or bathrooms could be made out of plasterboard, bookcases or metal and plastic screens. More often than not, though,
there was little or no division between separate rooms. Many of the early lofts were just multi-functional spaces

△ **A dining table
amongst oak and
brick in a classic
loft apartment.**

▷ **An intimate
dining area is
tucked away on
a lower level.**

with no more than a bed in one corner, a simple kitchen in another and a bath or shower plumbed into a third, perhaps with a curtain around it.

In a city where a conventional uptown apartment that could be afforded by the average avant-garde artist could scarcely hold an easel, the spaciousness of loft living was a wonderful indulgence. To divide up the space into smaller parts would have ruined the luxury of the open look and destroyed a space suited to work and play, to party nights and exhibitions, as well as to occasional communal living. Many of the industrial features of the early lofts were left as they were, treated as an intrinsic part of the look: exposed brick walls; ventilation tubes crisscrossing the ceiling; rough wooden or concrete floors and industrial-style strip lighting.

Now we know the loft look as a fully integrated part of mainstream city living, but many of the early loft lovers took up residence in a calculated defiance of convention. Some were squatters, others paid rent but had to keep quiet about the fact that they lived as well as worked in their lofts, as city planners refused for a long time to grant residential status to their buildings. For many, Andy Warhol's loft-style Factory summed up the subversive loft look of the 1960s: a space for painting, film making, life and loving. It was work and home. And in name and function, The Factory echoed Le Corbusier's idea of the house as "a machine for living."

The rise and rise of the loft look slowly began to transform SoHo, which over the decades shifted in status from a run-down Manhattan backwater to a creative hub. Slowly, others began to see the possibilities of loft living. Architects, closely followed by property developers, became fascinated by the open way of life and the relative ease with which spaces could be transformed into dramatic and enticing apartments. By the 1980s the loft was no longer a subversive space, but in danger of being overrun by Wall Street traders and urban professionals with money to burn on the fires of fashion raised by the growing band of loft developers. But the revolution soon evolved again and also spread its wings.

Since the mid-1980s the loft look has moved into a new era of sophistication and has tightened its grip upon countless cities, not just in the United States, but across Europe and into South America, Australia and

◁ **Contrasting textures add another dimension to this sophisticated living space, warmed by a neat inset fireplace.**

beyond. Every major city with a stock of old industrial buildings and warehouses ripe for redevelopment has seen a surge in loft living. The loft offers an open, contemporary home that satisfies both resident and architect. But it is also a model in recycling, where a redundant space is taken and transformed into something new. The loft has aided the revival of down-at-the-heels areas in many cities, not just New York's SoHo, but also Docklands and Southwark in London, or Castlefields in Manchester, as well as former industrialized zones in Barcelona, Chicago, Liverpool and Munich.

Now the loft revolution, with its open-plan and multi-functional style, its emphasis on light and contemporary design, has made its impact felt upon all kinds of urban space. The original definition of a loft has been stretched and pulled to include a mass of open-plan apartments in buildings old and new. Period homes are increasingly being reinvented and replanned in a way that allows a more open treatment of space. At the same time, new housing is being designed with a totally different set of priorities, taking on board some of the lessons of the Modernists and the searing impact of the loft revolution.

The contemporary urban home has also developed a new set of prerogatives that have only come to the fore in the past few years. Some of the early Modernists, like the staunch Minimalists of the 1980s and 90s who were drawn to the loft look, adopted a restrictive attitude to color, to pattern and to individual expression. Some loft developers took a similar stance, insisting on a design style that denied home owners many possibilities for individuality. Now, however, that has all changed and we recognize the value of individual expression, experimenting with color and texture, materials and finishes, in a way that goes beyond fashion or the dictates of architects and interior designers. We take the best aspects of the loft revolution, along with what we want of the Modernist example, and create our own urban spaces, where comfort, luxury and escapism are all vital and undeniable. And that is what this book is about — the best of city living and city style, where space and light are guiding principles in creating a home that is much more than a machine or a factory. It is a personal sanctuary, a retreat — an escape at the heart of the city.

▷ **Bamboo trees and a Japanese-style banner create an oriental flavor in a Victorian house reconfigured as a clean, contemporary space.**

space

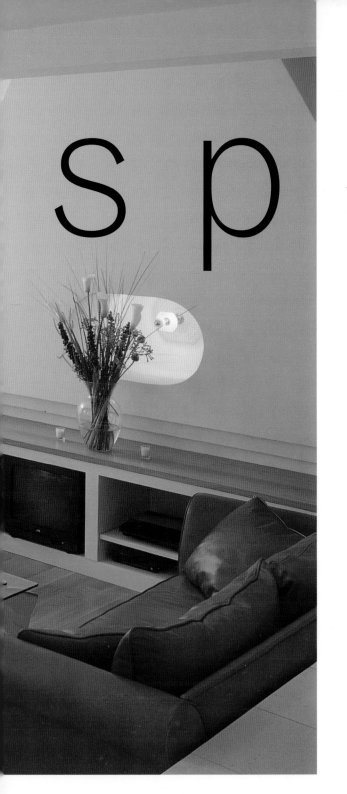

City life is fast and frenetic, enticing and energetic. We are drawn to the city because it lies at the center of things, as well as is rich in ideas and entertainment, opportunities and dreams. And we work and live in the metropolis because we want to make the best of its possibilities and convenient pleasures. But there is always a price to pay for city living and personal space, above all, is increasingly precious.

So much about the nature of city life today seems to deny us the room we need to breathe. We might travel to work in a rush-hour crush on the subway, do battle with our fellow passengers on the train, walk through a crowded underpass to our office and then find ourselves tied to a desk and a computer screen until the day eventually ends and we step back once again onto the subway.

In the city it is hard at times not to feel that our individuality is being undermined, and that we are simply part of a common mass moving from A to B.

That's why in our homes we need space above all else. We all need an individual escape from the everyday trials of working and traveling in the city crowds. We want space to indulge ourselves, to relax, to forget about the claustrophobia that city living can so often bring. This helps explain why the loft revolution has been so powerful and influential, setting in motion a movement towards open-plan rooms and light-filled interiors that now stretches across all kinds of urban space.

lofts

When loft living was born in the 1950s the attraction was obvious. It was space. For the Manhattan bohemians of SoHo the loft offered room enough for studio and home, mixing work, creativity and pleasure in one open-plan arrangement. These early lofts were often primitively styled. The space itself was so luxurious, so indulgent, that there was a limited amount of attention given to any other home comforts and seldom the money to pay for them. A bath might be plumbed right into the floor, a stove and fridge installed along a wall. The walls were simply left bare and exposed as hanging space for paintings and backdrops.

To fill a loft with a maze of walls and small rooms would have been to defeat the whole point of the space, especially in the eyes of the artists and writers drawn to those early versions of loft living. They both needed and wanted the open-plan arrangement and the light, setting a precedent that happened to coincide with the Modernist philosophy of open and informal living spaces. At the same

▷ **A dramatic, curving "hull" separates a mezzanine gallery – holding recessed relaxation and study rooms – from the main studio of this loft, with its high ceilings and swathes of sunlight.**

▽ **The unusually shaped furniture, in a mixture of fabrics and colors, is a main feature of the loft, each piece standing out to full effect in the open-plan scheme.**

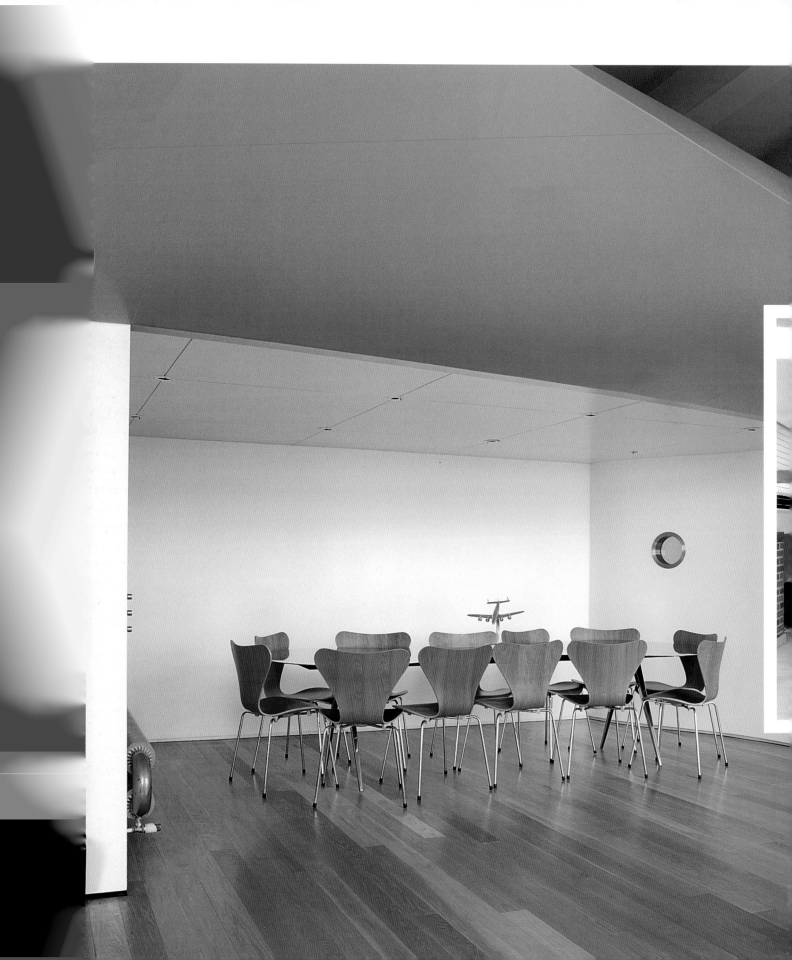

△ **Separate sleeping and dining zones are created using different floor levels, but without disturbing the open aesthetic.**

◁ **A dining zone has been partly tucked away under a gallery for a more enclosed feeling, yet it still benefits from the light of the main studio.**

time, however, the Modernist message was being complicated and even compromised by the wave of mass social housing projects and tower-block designs that Modernist architects such as Erno Goldfinger, Denys Lasdun, Mies van der Rohe and Le Corbusier embarked upon and that were soon labeled "Brutalist."

As former industrial spaces, the Manhattan lofts of the 1950s and 60s could seem hard and brutal urban environments themselves, and sometimes they were. With their banks of glass windows they could be too hot in summer and too cold in winter. They were not for families, nor were they for traditionalists or conservatives. But it was the space, the light and the potential that took loft design forwards, even as the Modernists began to be criticized and condemned for creating characterless new towers in the sky.

Ironically, the loft presented the acceptable face of Modernism, even though its origins were very separate from the calculated scheming of the great Modernist architects. The loft developed more organically, more naturally, based on the likes and dislikes

of those bohemian pioneers who began to colonize potential loft-style spaces within the shells of former industrial buildings.

As the New York loft look began to be taken up in the 1970s and 80s and moved slowly but surely towards mainstream acceptability, the model laid down for loft living by the SoHo pioneers was largely respected because it made sense, practically, aesthetically and instinctively. The property developers and their architects who worked on the first waves of commercial loft developments gambled that they could sell a whole new way of living along with the bricks, glass and steel.

Instead of a series of small rooms devoted to a single purpose – dining room, kitchen, living room and so on – the loft meant buying into the open-plan ideal. The concept of zoning was carried forward with built-in kitchen, dining and relaxation zones all created within the main room of the loft. Architects worked on different ways of partitioning off bedrooms and bathrooms, realizing that a completely open space with no privacy could be too much for a more mainstream market, especially families. They created a division between "public" and "private" rooms. The public space was the main open-plan room, the private space was the bedroom, the bathroom and perhaps a study.

Creating a private area within a loft space continues to be one of the major concerns for the designer and owner of any loft. The most common solution has been to section off a part of the shell to use either as a separate two-storey unit or gallery – making use of the double-height ceilings common to most loft spaces – while leaving the bulk of the main living space untouched. A typical two-level design might feature a bedroom up above, reached via a lightweight staircase, with a bathroom tucked underneath. Galleries or mezzanines would tuck away all the private rooms upstairs, keeping the space beneath for a recessed kitchen or dining area that opened out into the main living room. Whatever the solution, the idea was to interfere as little as possible with the proportions of the loft and allow light to stir right through the home.

△ **A curving,
unobtrusive wall
has been added
to one side of this
loft to enclose a
bedroom and
bathroom, with
gallery study
added above.**

◁ **A relaxation
area has been
created at one end
of this city loft
with a simple
arrangement of
sofas and coffee
table by the end
windows.**

The informality of the open-plan loft
style was in tune with the times. The
Modernists of the 1920s and 30s who
argued for a more relaxed and open
style of living were ahead of their age,
which was still clinging onto many
nineteenth-century values and ways
of living. But by the 1970s and 80s, as
the New York loft movement flour-
ished, there was an affluent genera-
tion ready and willing to adopt the
open-plan, loft lifestyle. Why have a
separate kitchen or dining room, as
long as the ventilation is good and the
space relaxing and easy? Why shut
yourself away to read a book or watch
the television? Loft living was no
longer bohemian.

From the 1980s onwards the loft look
has been refined as it has grown up
internationally, becoming increasingly

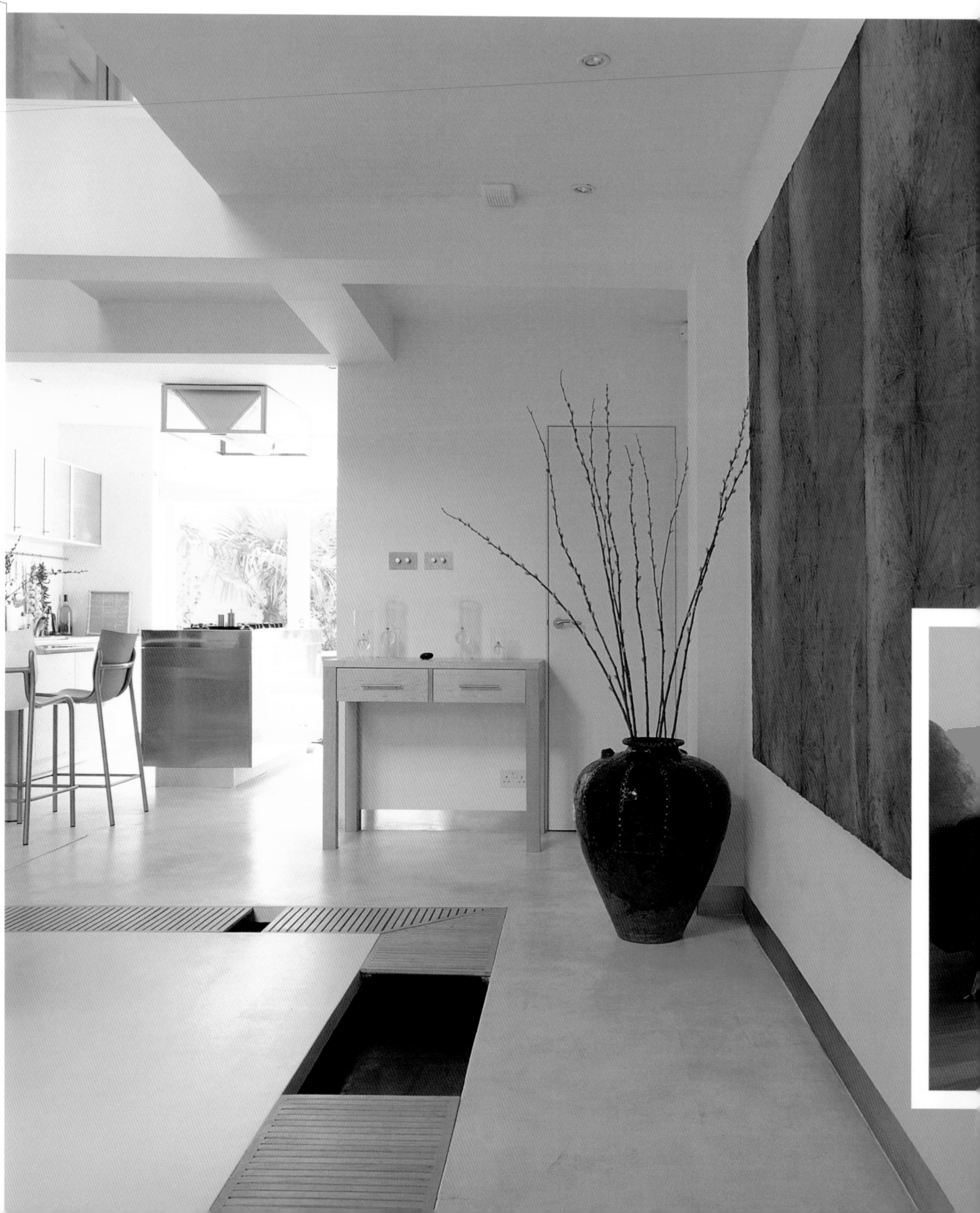

◁ **In the basement of this large period property, removing internal walls has created an open and inter-connecting dining and kitchen area, with a strong, through flow of light from the front to the back.**

▽ **Adding a carpet over a wooden floor helps separate off this comfort zone in one corner of a large studio space.**

sophisticated as solutions for separating public and private areas of the home have become ever more inventive. Many developers now offer a choice to loft buyers between owning a pre-fitted loft or simply getting hold of what is nothing more than an empty shell, with only the basic utilities piped in. The shell method has become common practice, as buyers demand the chance to stamp their own personality on their space and give free rein to their creative thinking.

The move towards the genuinely custom-made loft – which is very much in keeping with the individuality of the SoHo pioneers – offers greater flexibility in how to divide the overall space. The increased number of people who work at home means more home owners now want private work spaces, a place distinct from a main studio room, where one can leave work totally behind. A family will naturally want more private space than a single person, a keen cook will want a bigger kitchen than a fast-food addict. How to treat and separate living space has become a matter of choice founded on the freedom and flexibility of contemporary interior design.

zoning – public space

The loft revolution has sparked a reassessment of how we divide space. Without the need for a formal period-style layout – with dining room, nursery, parlor, kitchen, pantry, perhaps even servant's quarters – the idea of doing away with many of the home's traditional divisions has become

▽ **Varying floor
levels help separate
a side kitchen from
the main living area
of this studio room.**

▷ **A "private"
television and
comfort room lies
largely enclosed
and secluded within
this gallery space.**

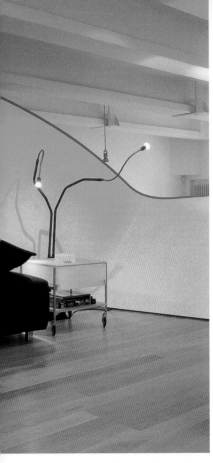

commonplace. In the public areas of a loft the whole concept of zoning has become an art in itself, creating separate areas within the main studio space without resorting to solid walls or permanent dividers that might undermine the loft's proportions and the natural flow of light.

A zone can be created simply and subtly, and in many different ways. Simply arranging a group of sofas and armchairs in one part of the studio can be enough to create a relaxation zone. Add a different texture for the flooring to define it further, perhaps a rug or a recessed area of carpet in an otherwise totally wooden or concrete floor. Different colors for the nearby walls of the differentiated zone also work well, as long as they don't interfere too much with the overall colorways of the studio itself.

For a more distinctive and effective separation of a zone, creating a step down to a recessed well area is a way of achieving an obviously separate area without any major changes to the loft itself. Even very small adjustments in floor level can be sufficient to create a sense of separation, while movable screens or even bookcases are a slightly more intrusive alternative, creating a light and impermanent wall.

Often the space itself will suggest its own divisions for zoning. The natural inclination in studio rooms is to position zones for relaxing and even entertaining close to windows and light sources, so pushing the kitchen to the back.

Many people are happy to see the kitchen as a fully integrated part of the public arena, which helps avoid cutting oneself off from partner, family or guests as you prepare and cook a meal. Others like to see some kind of separation, even if it is just a way to screen off the sight of pans piled in the sink and plates stacked on the work tops. Again, there are many possible solutions, but a favorite is the movable partition: a translucent Japanese-style

shoji screen or a glass panel that slides forwards and back to screen the kitchen – or perhaps a study area – from the main living room.

The development of loft style has helped discredit the idea that a partition has to be absolutely solid and fixed. Lightweight, movable screens in glass, Perspex, metal or wood can be fixed to tracks, runners or castors and easily swung into position. At its simplest, a partition might be a frosted panel of safety glass in a wooden frame, fixed to castors, to be wheeled in and out of position in an instant. More complex, but very sleek and effective, might be a series of tracked doors that swing out from side wall recesses to screen a kitchen or working area. Minimalists have partitioned whole rooms with cantilevered pivoting doors and sliding panels in a bid to hide the detritus of everyday life and screen off functional areas like kitchens and bathrooms when they are not in use.

For some, this kind of flexibility is not so much of an issue and they therefore have the option of using fixed alternatives for zoning that won't

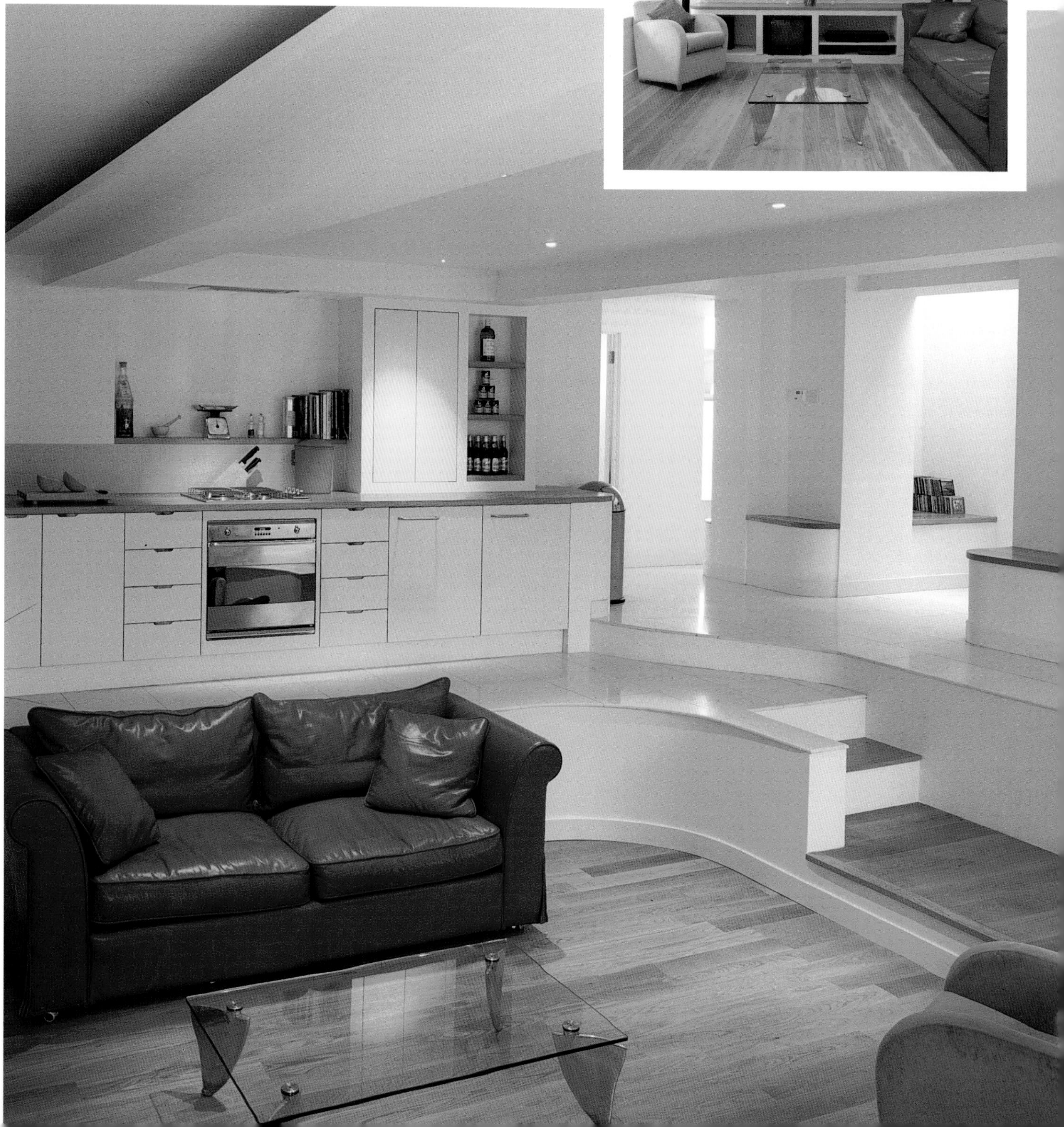

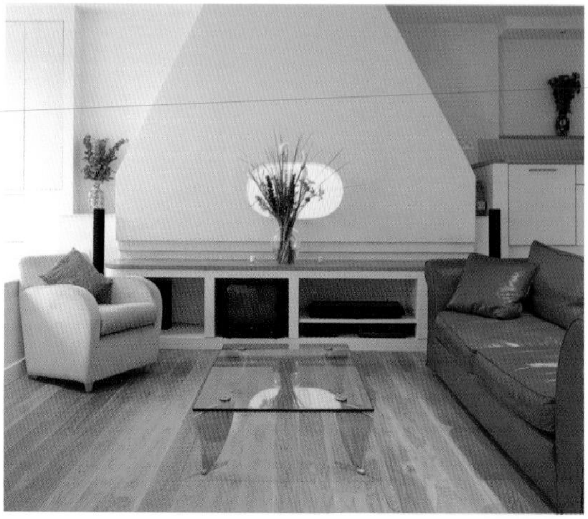

the "basement loft"

This basement-level apartment in the former boiler room of a old school was given a loft-style treatment by the owner of a PR company, who was partly inspired by the look of designer hotels like the Royalton in New York, with its gleaming Philippe Starck interiors.

△ **An old chimney creates a center-piece for the living room, with a central "fire" made of light for a feeling of hearth side.**

◁ **A sunken well in the main studio room offers a perfect relaxation and entertainment zone. The use of wooden flooring helps to further differentiate the area.**

▷ **Fluid lines for the ceiling and the curves of the "well" soften the harder, linear elements of the apartment.**

The owner was intrigued by the potential offered by an empty shell, which lay untaken as other parts of the surrounding metropolitan development were being snapped up. Yet there was also the possibility of extending the apartment's living space upwards from the basement by building on a small, spare patch of ground to the side of the old school building. This prompted her to finally take the risk of committing herself to the ambitious and sometimes difficult

job of creating a new home from what was little more than a hole in the ground.

In collaboration with her architects she came up with an innovative design that created a large, open-plan living space with a separate satellite bedroom and en-suite bathroom all on the same level. A thin, galley-style kitchen was run down one side of the main living room and a well was created on a lower-floor level to form a zone for relaxing and escapism. A bank of windows to the side of the main room opens out onto a sunken terrace, which sits way below ground level but still allows natural light to flood into the space, helping to overcome any suggestion of the claustrophobia usually found in basement apartments.

Creating the well in the main room, experimenting with different floor levels and softening the ceiling with recessed downlighters and an undulating profile – which makes a feature of the roof beams – means that the space seems large and airy, but also soft and pleasant to the eye, with any hard edges diffused with curving lines. The old chimney unit was utilized as an architectural feature in itself, a reminder of the apartment's original function as well as a dramatic centerpiece with a "fire" made of light at its heart.

Moving up a stairway to the side of the main room, a dining room was added to a new-build section of the apartment, along with a beautifully impactive and indulgent bathroom located just inside the old boys' entrance gateway of the school, and which used the stone doorway as part of the design scheme. Blue mosaic tiles for an inset, custom-made concrete bath – its weight supported by extra beams beneath – and a panel of luminescent, blue glass miniature windows stand out against the white walls and white Spanish limestone for the floors.

Moving upstairs again onto another new-build level, a second bedroom was created with a large porthole window to one side and French windows to the other, leading to a small balcony. The room is thus filled with light from both sides. Extending the apartment on so many different levels has not only increased the sense of space, but created opportunities to promote the circulating light.

White walls throughout, along with the choice of materials such as limestone and light oak floors, means that sunlight can bounce through the space while splashes of color in fabrics for the armchairs, the warm glow of leather for the sofa and the use of handpainted sea-blue glass help add character and warmth. Lighting plans throughout – which mix downlighters and character ceiling lights – have been carefully engineered to offer a choice of ambient light for day or evening, with the flexibility of dimmer switches.

This is an apartment that has been put together with an emphasis not just on space, but also comfort and luxury. It comes together in a cohesive, confident whole – despite being located on many different levels – because of the clarity and restraint of the design. It offers an example of how the unlikeliest of spaces can be transformed with imagination and integrity.

◁ **White limestone floors and white walls throughout most of the apartment create unity, even across junctions to private spaces like the bedroom.**

◁ **A dining room was created on ground-floor level while the entrance to the bathroom uses the original boys' gateway to the old Victorian school.**

▽ **The internal windows of stained glass in the bathroom are a decorative centerpiece that also allows light to filter through from a hallway atrium beyond.**

erode the basic space too severely. The half-height wall is the classic example – a light panel cantilevered to the floor that still allows light to circulate above and to the sides. In wood, or better still in glass, a fixed panel can seem simply to float like a monolith while screening the most functional parts of a kitchen, the mess of chil-

dren's toys in a playroom or the files and papers of a work area.

It is also important to get away from the misapprehension that a divider – or even a fixed, solid wall – has to be linear and precise. Some of the most interesting loft designs have a more fluid profile, introducing curves and undulating lines to help soften the

hard, straight lines found in the basic structure of loft shells.

Whatever the choice, zoning is something to be approached with restraint and a light touch, in a loft or any open-plan environment. The glory of the studio clearly lies in its very openness. Interfering too much with panels, partitions and banks of furniture is, of course, to take away the whole point of open-plan living.

zoning – private space

It is obvious and true that open living is part of the nature of loft style, where the whole home is treated as an escape. But most of us find it hard to feel at ease without at least some element of privacy, especially at times when we are feeling at our most vulnerable. The contemporary loft, unlike some of its more extreme Manhattan forbears, takes account of the need for private as well as public zones in the home.

Bedrooms and bathrooms are usually separated off from the loft's main studio. Sometimes that means a mezzanine, where the floor-to-ceiling height of the private space is cut

◁ **The use of a warmer color and flooring treatment in the recessed bedrooms of this loft provides a welcoming, private retreat.**

◁ **This attic-style bedroom is separated from other living spaces by a monolith wall that stops short of the ceiling, allowing light to spill over.**

▽ **A light tubular staircase spirals up to a mezzanine, providing easy access without intruding on the dimensions of the loft.**

down for a greater sense of intimacy. Lightweight or cantilevered stairs provide unobtrusive access leading up to the separated space, although using glass walls and internal windows can allow light to flow right through to recessed rooms positioned to the back or side of a loft-style home. Alternatively, private rooms may sit one on top of the other in a sectioned-off part of the main loft, with a stairway hidden away within the private zone itself.

Either way, even in private space there's no need to assume that traditional divisions are necessarily the best. If the main bedroom has an opportunity for an en-suite bathroom, for instance, it may be more of an indulgence and a luxury to find a way to connect the two without using any

△ **Bedrooms deserve a more indulgent and personal approach than any other room in the home. They must be a sanctuary.**

◁ **Bedroom clutter is hidden behind folding screens, while the area is softened and warmed by the bold purple of the pillows.**

solid walls or doorways. The formality that demands we separate ourselves from our partners as we bathe is a thing of the past, although a guest bathroom may well demand a more conservative approach.

As with zoning and the general design of any home, it is important to think how you want to use the space, as well as what might be stylish, practical and affordable. A guest bedroom, for one, can be wasted space for much of the year. Creating a multi-functional room that can double up as a study or playroom is relatively simple, all the more effective if the right storage and furniture is considered, so as to hide away the everyday clutter when the space turns back into a bedroom. Fold-away beds or futons, meanwhile, make the transition from one to the other more practical and complete.

The main bedroom, though, has to be the true sanctuary. The cliché says that the kitchen is the heart of the home, but the truth of the saying has been eaten away by the fact that for many metropolitans the kitchen is seldom used for more than making a bowl of cereal from one week to the next. It is the bedroom that has to be the real heart of the home, a place where we really can relax and escape, one of our most private places where the statistics famously tell us we spend – or should spend – up to a third of our lives.

The bedroom has to be a haven. It needs to be warmer and less exposed than other areas. Comfort has to come first, even above style. That often calls for a different treatment in terms of color and finishes than the rest of the home, one that aims to soften and personalize the room as well as add a more sensual note. The bedroom is the one place where luxuries really are quite excusable, from a built-in television to a recessed, walk-in dressing room. The bedroom should be a room you want to spend time in, not a cell or a tomb.

apartments

The impact of the loft look has spread far beyond the loft itself. Many new conversions of defunct office blocks, hospitals, banks and other urban environments have taken the lessons of

loft style to heart and worked to promote a healthy sense of space and sunlight. New-build apartment blocks created on brownfield sites in many cities have tried to re-create some of the glamour and feel of the original lofts, while helping reclaim and resurrect neglected parts of the metropolis.

There has also been a real shift in the way developers, architects and designers think about apartments in general. From the 1960s to the 1980s, just as the loft look was coming to life in New York, it was common to find a very different approach to apartment spaces. With demand for urban homes outstripping supply, a breed of builders and developers in cities like London, Paris, Madrid and even Manhattan itself took a very short-term, greed-fueled approach to creating apartments. Grand period homes were divided up recklessly, with a whole sequence of claustrophobic boxes crammed into too small a volume. In apartment blocks, building regulations were neglected as spacious apartments were sub-divided, ruining the original proportions and scale of many homes.

Now, partly as a result of the rise and rise of loft style, there's a recognition that more value will be placed on apartments that do have a feeling of space and light, and that simply dividing up rooms to create miniature extra bedrooms is not so much creating an attractive home as forming a cell block. A developer or construction company can now make more of a profit by concentrating on proportion, detail and finishing rather than on simply boxing off as many units as possible. And in many countries building restrictions have become stricter and have been enforced to a greater degree, although there is still a long way to go to prevent abuses to space and architecture.

Throughout the 1990s and into the new century, apartment owners and developers have been working to correct mistakes made by the short-sited in the decades before. Partly as a result of the renewed emphasis on light and open-plan living, partly as a result of a shortage of larger and family-oriented city-center homes, small apartments are constantly being combined to form a spacious

whole, often restoring the original proportions of the space. Sub-divided houses are slowly being reclaimed in part or in their entirety as home owners buy up other apartments around them and extend their living space, often in a very open and modern style that makes the most of contemporary materials.

Many existing single apartments are also being reconsidered, with an eye on how best to eliminate claustrophobia and open up the space as much as possible.

This might be done by nothing more complicated than removing an unnecessary doorway, or replacing a wooden door with another made of safety glass to allow light to filter through from room to room. The fact that reinforced steel joists (RSJs) can often be used to take the structural load off a brick or block wall has also meant that doorways can be enlarged with relative ease and walls removed, or perhaps replaced by glass or flexible partitions.

Naturally, any structural changes of this kind, even minor changes, need to be carefully thought through. It is

△ **This dining table has been positioned by a window for a reassuring flow of natural light.**

◁ **A change in floor level separates this kitchen and relaxation zone, with furniture facing away from the cooking area.**

◁ In large loft spaces distinct areas for dining and relaxing can quite easily be created without upsetting the basic luxury of open living.

common sense and common practice to consult a structural engineer, and very often an architect as well, before going ahead with any alterations that might involve load-bearing walls. There may well be other issues that complicate the changes you want to make – perhaps there is pipework or cabling running through the walls that may need to be diverted. In some cases planning consent may be required and building regulations will need to be followed.

Yet even small alterations can have a real impact. Adding skylights or enlarging doorways and windows can transform an oppressive space into something very different and desirable. The openness of loft style might well be applicable to a more modest apartment, creating a welcoming studio-style space.

For a lighter approach to existing divisions solid walls might be replaced, or partially replaced, with translucent screens or glass blocks. Often the ideal solution is to try to get at least some element of light flowing right through the space from the front to the back of the unit.

The message of open urban living is not to take what you have or what you are given for granted. Many converted apartments in period blocks and the rooms within them were created by adding little more than hardboard walls in the first place, so it may be simpler than you think to adjust or remove those divisions. A pair of small, impractical rooms might be easily combined to create a better sense of proportion and allow for a more dramatic and stirring bedroom or bathroom. Badly positioned banks of fitted cupboards might be removed or repositioned to allow a greater sense of spaciousness in a key room, or ceilings raised in top-floor apartments as an alternative way of enlarging dimensions.

Much of the skill of creating interiors that work lies in seeing beyond surface elements like color, fabric and finishes to these fundamental issues of proportion, scale and light. Getting the basic space correct means that all else should follow and fit into place, but trying to get an apartment right when the basics are obviously wrong is to fight a losing battle.

◁ **A kitchen – complete with heavy-duty extractor fans – has been neatly positioned at the far end of this loft to be integral but not intrusive.**

houses

Period town houses were traditionally sub-divided into a whole series of small rooms for many reasons. This was partly due to a formal lifestyle, with each room assigned a clearly defined function. But it was also due to conserving heat. Modestly sized rooms were thought to retain warmth far more effectively than large spaces, so the tendency was towards intimate proportions with fireplaces dotted throughout the rooms, bedrooms and reception rooms alike.

In other words, many of the houses we choose to live in today were designed on the basis of an outdated set of needs and requirements. Today we no longer have the same desire for formal, private spaces. Advances in heating, energy conservation and insulation mean we should never have to worry about opening up spaces for fear of simply being too cold. We now demand light and space, but are often still drawn to the appealing character of period houses.

The solutions have sometimes been profound and complex. Most period homes built before the 1900s, and some built since, will have a network of internal load-bearing brick or stone walls. This makes any restructuring with the aim of opening up the internal space a matter for engineers and architects. But with the use of RSJs and steel lintels or cages the traditional layout of a period home can be reinvented to maximize light and proportion.

The most dramatic reconfigurations of period homes have involved erecting steel cages that allow the basic structure of the house to be supported from the four sides of the building, taking the load away from most internal supports. This gives the freedom to completely reinvent the layout of the rooms, even removing floors to create double-height areas in the home. It is almost like starting again, redrawing a floor plan to suit a more contemporary lifestyle and aesthetic.

Complete structural upheaval, however, is a massive undertaking. It means talking very closely to architects and engineers to see what can be done and looking closely at the work of a number of architects with direct experience of the look and style

a contemporary family home

The remodeling of a city-center apartment in this six-storey, nineteenth-century building created an airy home for a young, cosmopolitan family. Interior designer Charles Bateson's brief was to provide a contemporary look that gave a better sense of space and light, achieved with a minimum of structural change.

The greatest challenge in reinventing the apartment was to undo a feeling of enclosure in the main room, where a heavy oak staircase leading up to a mezzanine gallery above destroyed the true proportions of the area and created an obstacle the moment anyone entered the room. The staircase was removed and replaced with a steel and glass design cantilevered to the wall, so light that it barely intruded into the space below. Heavy balustrading around the gallery was also replaced by a glass balcony, allowing daylight to filter right across from the mezzanine windows.

Another problem was that the top of the building's elevator shaft stretched right up into the gallery and almost divided it in two, with a platform a few feet from the ground that threatened to make the room redundant. The solution was to design an elegant built-in desk right on top of the shaft, creating a spacious study rich in sunlight, yet with the feeling of an isolated retreat from the rest of the apartment.

Choices in color and texture give a natural sense of unity to the living room. The existing parquet floor was stripped and lightened, with a broad loom carpet cut into a rug to create a contrast underneath the seating area. The limestone fireplace and stone colors for the walls, and the white for the ceiling, all create a neutral backdrop that brings the best out of the earthy shades of the upholstered furniture. Added contrast comes with velvet cushions, a raffia-like

▷ **The mezzanine study has been fitted with a wealth of storage, while light filters effectively through the glass balcony.**

△ **The gallery provides welcome extra space without intruding on the open, airy quality of the living room below.**

◁ **The glass and steel staircase to the mezzanine is light enough to be unobtrusive and takes up very little space.**

▷ **Close positioning of the furniture around the fireplace creates a more intimate area within the main living room.**

covering for the chaise longue, and the dark green and brown check for the ottoman. For the windows, heavy curtains were replaced by a new idea: linen curtains on a neat and continuous track running right across the wall, with a light set of blinds also tucked tight into the windows themselves, offering alternatives for shrouding and accentuating both natural light and intimacy.

The adjoining entrance hallway was another problem, being far too unwelcoming and dark. A bank of wall mirrors was placed opposite the front door, creating an illusion of space and also increasing light levels. Recessed downlighters throughout much of the apartment give the basic source of artificial light, with lamps added for consoles and tables as well as the occasional wall light.

The dining room was treated very differently, to create a more atmospheric and individual space. Wallpaper with the grained look of wood was cut into squares and laid in a geometric block pattern for an unusual and contemporary feel. The colors chosen for upholstery and curtains were darker than for most of the other rooms in the apartment. Candlelight throws a flickering warmth across the walls.

With the bedrooms, the emphasis shifts back towards a neutral color palette, but with some dramatic surprises and juxtapositions. In the main bedroom, for instance, an oversized headboard becomes a centerpoint through its sheer size and the warmth of the leather and sycamore materials that stand out against the creamy, off-white tones of the walls. On the opposite wall an abstract red oil painting above a low wooden chest of drawers stands out as a flash of bright color.

△ **In the entrance hallway a mirrored wall gives an illusion of spaciousness over a limited floor area.**

▷ **One of the more modest rooms in the apartment became the dining room. The emphasis is on warmth and indulgence.**

△ **The crimson shades of the artwork stand out in the bedroom, offering a more sensual note.**

In the white attic bedroom a slightly different approach is taken, one which accentuates the light that filters in from the French windows that lead to a small roof balcony. Shades of white for walls, linen and headboards, along with stone and earthy shades for carpet, bedside tables and rattan chairs, create a simple but effective scheme that ties together perfectly.

Here, as elsewhere through the home, the openness of the space is helped by large windows and access to outside areas, with terraced external rooms offering a connection with the outdoors and a rooftop view across the city landscape. Even these relatively limited bursts of outdoor space add to the overall feeling of wellbeing in the home and offer extra opportunities for summer living and entertaining in the fresh air.

you are considering. It is advisable to visit some of their other projects, perhaps even talk to some of the home owners who have taken similar steps, before settling on one professional. Always establish the parameters of the job and the extent to which the architect will be involved in both planning and supervising the work. Establish as clearly as possible an estimate of the costs, allowing a significant leeway for unforeseen problems. The results can be quite wonderful, combining many of the charms of the period home with a very open, airy and modern look. Occasionally, however, your research may bring the realization that it is in fact more sensible, practical and cheaper to move on to somewhere that better suits the way you want to live. Or even build from scratch.

Complete reconfiguration represents the extreme end of the scale. There are many possibilities for reworking a period home that has a traditional room layout without setting off on such a drastic course of action. Again, the key is to think about what you want to use the space for and the balance you seek between public and private places within the home.

Most commonly, it is the main reception rooms of the house that are reconfigured or adjusted. A separate living room with a dining room behind can often be combined with relative ease using RSJ supports, either by creating a double doorway to link the two rooms or by removing much of the wall to create one large space, with light moving freely between the two. Other small box rooms may deserve a similar treatment to create more enticing spaces, and it might be possible to enlarge existing windows or doorways. In period homes, the attic and roof space is a common area for expansion, allowing you to create a loft in miniature at the top of the house – complete with banks of skylights – for use as a main bedroom or a study. If the house is being extended at the rear, perhaps the extension can be used to open up existing areas, with a glasshouse arrangement to allow extra light right into the home.

Yet much can be done towards opening up a period home without

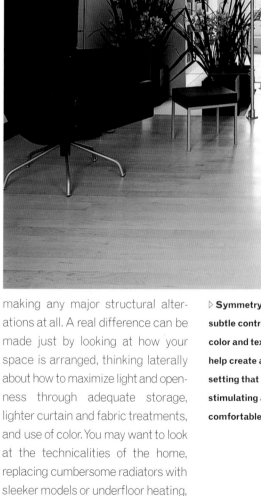

making any major structural alterations at all. A real difference can be made just by looking at how your space is arranged, thinking laterally about how to maximize light and openness through adequate storage, lighter curtain and fabric treatments, and use of color. You may want to look at the technicalities of the home, replacing cumbersome radiators with sleeker models or underfloor heating, for instance, or perhaps relocating boilers and water tanks if they are in any way intrusive.

▷ **Symmetry and subtle contrasts in color and texture help create a setting that is both stimulating and comfortable.**

◁ **This L-shaped room offers a natural division between two seating areas, one more enclosed than the other.**

Simply reconsidering the use of a room can make a difference. If an area, such as a guest room or study, is seldom used but forms one of the brightest rooms in the house, then think about switching its role with a main bedroom or a living room. Don't be ruled by convention – if the upstairs rooms are lighter and better for entertaining or relaxing, then take your main living spaces upwards. Every step is geared towards maximizing the openness of the urban home, taking the example of loft living with all of its benefits and looking at how to apply this in a very different context.

new-builds

Building from scratch is the ultimate dream, but increasingly difficult in most major cities, where every scrap of building land is a prize. With new-build, of course, the possibilities are endless and the direction and emphasis of the design a matter of choice. The only limitations on your freedom of design lie in planning restrictions and the limits of imagination and bank balance. Just be sure of your architect and don't be tempted to allow him or

her to run away with his or her own statement. The home is a personal refuge too – any good architect will respect clients who are able to express clear ideas, within a constructive dialogue, about exactly what they want out of their perfect urban home.

Yet building from nothing can sometimes be cheaper and more cost effective than you might expect. And without many of the constraints presented by converting an existing period property there is a valuable liberty in choosing floor plans and materials to suit the way you want to live. The influence of open-plan design style has revolutionized the way in which many homes are being built, with an appreciation of the informality of contemporary lifestyles and of the necessity for space and light. It took much of the last century to adapt to a new set of priorities in the design of the home and to shake off the stifling legacy of traditional period style. But now that we have done so there is an undeniable sense of excitement in creating urban homes where convention and claustrophobia are obsolete and innovation, creativity and comfort are everything.

light

Light is a basic need, an ingredient of life. It has a profound effect upon our health, our well-being and our state of mind. The way early building methods developed in the West often denied light, for many different reasons, but now the provision and encouragement of light is seen as one the basic tenets of any architect's work. The Modernist godfather Le Corbusier famously described the home as "a receptacle for light and sun," words that have been seized upon with a religious fervor by architects and interior designers alike.

Yet this widespread acceptance of the essential need for light in the home is a surprisingly recent development. Houses and apartments across our cities are often seriously deficient in this most obvious of necessities. Even some homes that were built as little as 30 or 40 years ago can appear gloomy and lifeless. Providing space without light is a contradiction in terms and, as the Modernists argued and the loft revolution proved, the two simply have to go hand in hand. Light destroys claustrophobia, transforms dull and inhibitive areas and lifts color and texture to a point of clarity and quality.

It is sometimes assumed that artificial lighting can offer a ready-made solution to the problems of an obscure and shadowy space. However, artificial light is not a solution in itself – despite the many advances in the technology and creativity of lighting designers – and has to be used to complement natural light without attempting to replace or overrule it. Natural light and artificial light should work hand in hand, but nature always has to come first.

natural light

At its best modern architecture uses natural light as an intrinsic part of the design of the home. Light has a fundamental creative purpose, as well as a practical appeal, accentuating the form and line of the interior, throwing patterns of sunshine across walls and floors. For Modernists such as Alvar Aalto, Richard Neutra and Philip Johnson, or contemporary masters such as Richard Rogers, Norman Foster and Tadao Ando, light has been the key to architectural brilliance and innovation, treated as a priority and never forgotten.

Yet one of the side effects of the surge in demand for urban housing that took place between the 1960s and 1980s was the erosion of the natural resource of light, which was already in short supply. Across the urban landscape, where we often live and work in the shadows, it is all the more important to consider and promote natural light. But construction companies, developers and architects have often been lured into designs for the home that pay little or no consideration to light, just volume. Walk into such a

△ **Shafts of natural light lift the terracotta of this chaise longue and help warm the room in an airy ground-floor apartment.**

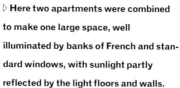

▷ **Here two apartments were combined to make one large space, well illuminated by banks of French and standard windows, with sunlight partly reflected by the light floors and walls.**

▷ **Sunlight lifts the colors of ceramics and glass, helping to promote contrasts in texture and tone.**

home and you can instinctively see that without adequate sources of natural light the space just doesn't work, that it has no vision, no character and no charm.

Little wonder, then, that so many of the changes and improvements made to houses and apartments have concentrated on simply lifting the level of natural light, changes inspired by the alluring example of the loft, with its floor-to-ceiling windows and where light comes as a given necessity. Many structural alterations to existing homes are put in motion with the dual aim of increasing both space and light, and it is true that simply opening up the dimensions of an interior will often promote the flow of sunlight. But it may be – especially with darker spaces such as basements or homes where light is restricted by trees or buildings – that you need to think more carefully and constructively about maximizing natural sunlight.

It pays to look at how the light actually works in your home. Depending on the direction your home is facing, depending on the seasons, depending on location, light levels can vary con-

siderably. See if you can apply any simple, common-sense steps to improve the flow of light. Avoid positioning any tall or obstructive furniture by windows, clear window sills of books and clutter, and, if you have heavy curtains, for instance, look at replacing them with blinds or shutters. Or even remove them altogether.

The whole approach to window treatments has shifted over recent years towards a very minimalist look, in keeping with a contemporary style that veers away from heavy fabrics and complicated layers of material. The use of bunches of fabric – as with the use of divisive, traditional floor plans for period homes – stems from an outmoded approach to design. With improvements in heating and glazing there should no longer be any need for heavy curtains that once formed extra layers of insulation. If heat loss is a worry, then consider improving window frames and glass rather than blocking out valuable sources of light with barriers and blocks of expensive fabrics that will usually be restrictive to some extent, even when tied back.

△ **Translucent window blinds fitted tight into the frames allow light to percolate through, even when lowered for protection against high summer sun.**

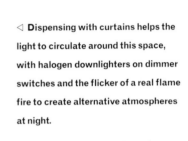

◁ **Dispensing with curtains helps the light to circulate around this space, with halogen downlighters on dimmer switches and the flicker of a real flame fire to create alternative atmospheres at night.**

▽ **Alternate light sources offer flexibility in creating different moods. Here there is good natural light plus the option of downlighters or a single, warm tungsten ceiling light over the dining table.**

▷ **Skylights can be one of the simplest and most effective additions to homes with available roof space.**

▷ **French windows open onto a small balcony. A light window treatment offers privacy without being obstructive.**

If privacy is an issue then consider lighter curtain fabrics that have some degree of translucence to allow light to filter through, perhaps lightly woven linens or cottons, such as fine muslin. Replacing normal glass with opaque, frosted or colored glass on lower-window levels, where you feel the need to screen off the outside world, is another common alternative to curtains. Frosted window glass – together with countless variations in blinds and shutters – are common to city lofts, where some degree of privacy is generally needed. Loft style usually rejects solid barriers of curtain fabric, as they tend to go against the simplicity and restraint of the overall design. Half-height shutters made with frosted glass or Perspex might offer a perfect solution to the privacy problem, giving an instant choice between transparent and opaque windows, which will allow light to filter through either way.

It may be desirable to enlarge or extend existing windows, depending on the planning restrictions in force and on any structural considerations. Skylights are one of the most popular and common window additions to homes and apartments where there is accessible roof space, as direct light shining in from above is always more effective than light that filters in from the side of a room.

Internally, there are many structural and spatial possibilities for improving the flow of light, yet simply taking a door off its hinges where you can do without it is one of the simplest ways of promoting the flow of light. Glass doors – transparent or opaque – are another simple option, while internal windows or panels are effective but clearly rather more complex. French windows to any outside space are in wide currency and for good reason. Choosing light and reflective surface

case study

a light-enriched space

Designed by a young architect as a home for himself, this light-enriched space is part of a modestly sized city-center development. Built from scratch, it forms a bachelor home, with two bedrooms on the ground floor below the main loft-style studio.

The moment you walk into this house, the impression is one of openness, with sunlight playing across the floor in parallelogram shapes formed by banks of side windows and recessed skylights. Despite being in a very busy, urban area the feeling is one of tranquillity, with a calming connection to green space provided by the largest windows in the studio, which slide back and open onto a small balcony, overlooking gardens and walkways below.

Most of the light for the studio, through necessity, has to come from one side of the room. Yet effective design solutions mean that this fact hardly even registers. Instead of simply creating one seamless wall of sheet glass, the architect used a number of different window treatments to help break up the space and make it more visually stimulating. At the more secluded end of the house stand the French windows and balcony, plus one other full-height window. Towards the more exposed end of the studio, closer to nearby streets, there is a sequence of six smaller square windows, supplemented by skylights to the two edges of the roof which throw a strong cast of sunshine down into the studio. Through a door to the far end of this main room extra daylight seeps in from the kitchen, which has its own bank of windows.

The smaller portals are kept bare while translucent blinds positioned tight into the frames offer an option of privacy for

▷ **The mix of skylights, French windows and side lights creates a rich, revolving pattern of sunlight playing through the main room and over the pale oak floors.**

▷ **Smaller windows are left bare and simple to maximize their effectiveness.**

△ French windows
to one side of the
dining table open
onto a small
balcony, overlook-
ing gardens and
walkways below.

◁ **The skylights to either side of the room create strong, seductive pulses of sunlight. Natural light is at its strongest and most effective shining into the home directly from above.**

▷ **Light, reflective surfaces such as glass, steel and birch help reflect light – natural and artificial – in the kitchen.**

the largest windows, without being intrusive or blocking out valuable daylight. A dozen recessed halogen downlighters, in lines of six, provide ambient artificial light without disturbing the clean lines of the ceiling. Most surfaces are light and reflective, with white for the walls and pale oak for the floors. Furniture and upholstery in light or earthy shades fit in with the natural-color palette, with a number of chairs by Swedish Modernist architect and furniture designer Bruno Matthson that are very much in keeping with the sleek, contemporary aesthetic.

Books and files are stored neatly in banks of shelves to the side while the kitchen features plenty of storage space to hide away cooking implements and laundry machines. Glass wall tiles, steel work tops and birch ply cupboards juxtapose industrial-style materials with natural finishes.

The house is an example of how to use the lightest areas of the home as the main living space, with the bedrooms tucked away downstairs. It may be in defiance of Western convention, yet it clearly makes sense to use the brightest parts of the building – which often tend to be on the upper floors – as the key rooms.

A curving concrete staircase – illuminated by another semi-circular skylight above – runs down from the studio to the bedrooms and bathroom. In the main bedroom natural light is maximized with French windows while a dramatic curving wall of glass bricks separates the bedroom from the bathroom, allowing light to percolate between the two. With the bathroom lights switched on the whole shower cubicle glows like a giant lantern while downlighters and two bedside lights supplement the effect.

◁ The translucent
drum of this glass
shower cubicle has
a warm iridescent
glow when the
bathroom lights
are on.

materials and colors will always help promote natural light.

The use of mirrored tiles, too, both for creating an illusion of space and refracting light, is coming back into fashion for walls and ceilings. Wall mirrors, similarly, are more than decorative and larger versions can promote a sense of light and space as well as being centerpieces in themselves.

From minor steps to major solutions, encouraging natural light makes an important difference to the urban home. Light helps create a feeling of warmth, of welcome. Light can often

be the key to creating an effective urban environment.

artificial light

Since Thomas Edison came up with the incandescent light bulb in 1879 artificial light has completely changed the way we live, transforming both the city and the home. It has given us the freedom to live according to our own clocks, rather than to the natural order set by the rise and fall of the sun. It might seem strange that while so much else has moved on, the basic design of the incandescent tungsten

filament bulb has changed so little since the first mass-produced bulbs were put on the market early in the twentieth century. But the tungsten bulb is the exception to the rule. Lighting technology is ever changing. Think of how quickly halogen bulbs have become common currency, how fiber optics have come into the mainstream.

Innovative lighting has long been closely related to modern architectural interior design. Designers and architects such as Ettore Sotsass, Alvar Aalto and Eileen Gray were not only fascinated by the possibilities of artificial light, but turned to lighting design themselves, as have many contemporary designers such as Philippe Starck, Ron Arad and Jasper Morrison. There has always been an inescapable modernity to lighting design and the feeling that lighting is at the cutting edge of design continues to be alluring.

Attempts to cloak ceiling lights and lamps in fabrics and frills—to put a traditional spin on such a new medium—have never seemed particularly convincing. Reflective metals, translucent

▷ A pair of wall
lights on either
side of the fireplace
provide a warm
tungsten glow,
supplemented by
table lamps.

▷ **Bedside lamps throw a warm cast of tungsten light over the walls and ceiling, softening the whites and creams of the bedroom.**

◁ **Recessed halogen downlighters are tucked away neatly, without disturbing the smooth lines of the apartment.**

glass and other modern, semi-industrial materials have always seemed more appropriate, with many Deco chrome and Lalique shades of the 1920s and 30s appearing quite contemporary even now.

sources of light

Today there are three basic kinds of lighting source: tungsten, halogen and fluorescent. Incandescent tungsten filament bulbs have a familiar, warm, yellow-orange glow to them and still form the most commonly used domestic bulb. The warmth of the light thrown out by tungsten makes it popular for ambient background lighting, although it still has a place as workhorse illumination in the form of desk lamps or tracked spotlights.

Halogen bulbs (or tungsten halogen) create a cool, crisp, bright illumination that is the closest form of artificial light we have to natural daylight. Ever since halogen bulbs were miniaturized in the 1970s and became more flexible in their application, there has been a far greater use of halogen, which is now the source of choice for the majority of interior designers and architects. Halogen lamps can be very discreet and unobtrusive, which is part of their attraction, and are commonly used as recessed downlighters, supplying the key artificial light in the home. Standard-voltage halogen lighting can also be dimmed, as well as isolated in various different zones to give greater control and flexibility. Low-voltage halogen bulbs, which need a transformer to adapt from standard voltage, can be smaller still and even more discreet, giving narrow beams of light.

Fluorescent lighting, long known as neon, was first introduced in the 1930s. Neon formed the classic colored and shaped signage of pre-war Manhattan and many other cities. It has long had industrial and commercial connotations, partly because harsh fluorescent strip lighting found its way into every hospital, school and public institution you care to name in the 1960s and 70s.

Fluorescent lighting has been virtually discredited in the past, not just for being unflattering to the skin, or for its bluish tinge, but for its characteristic pulsing quality, which has been blamed – rightly or wrongly – for causing sensory discomfort.

▷ **Fluorescent task lighting tucked under kitchen cabinets illuminates work surfaces.**

Yet fluorescent lighting has been all but reinvented over the past decade and is now making its presence felt again, with the flickering largely eliminated. Miniature strip lights are commonly used in kitchens as functional lighting, discreetly attached to the bottom of cupboard units, throwing a practical glow of cool light over work surfaces. The fact that some fluorescent lighting can now be operated on dimmer switches, and the possibility it offers for colored tubes, has helped give it a far more enticing versatility.

Other more specific and specialist sources of light find their way into the home through character plug-in lamps of all kinds. Fiber optic lights enjoy a growing appeal – although they can be surprisingly expensive – and are gradually being used more experimentally for domestic applications. Semi-industrial or street-style lighting such as metal-halide and sodium rarely find their way into the home, although metal-halide lighting is sometimes used as a heavy-duty light for gardens and other outside spaces, as it is said to be close to natural daylight, and can encourage plant growth.

Lights form design features, to be chosen in sympathy with the style of the home.

Artistry connects with practicality in new-generation wall lights.

At the other end of the technology scale is candlelight and natural flame. Primitive but timelessly seductive, the soft flicker of candlelight adds instant charm and atmosphere to a room while the caress of a flaming fire – using either solid fuel or a gas equivalent – throws shadows and a glowing light around a space. We are naturally drawn to a fireside, as we are instinctively drawn to any light, and a real fire can be very reassuring while helping to soften the harder edges of a room. The design of fires and fire surrounds has moved on with the times and

there are plenty of designs with a very contemporary feel available. Fire retardant surrounds and fire guards should always be used where there is a real flame, to ensure safety. Adequate ventilation is also important.

uses of light

Creating lighting plans has become an increasingly exact and sophisticated science. Many home owners declare themselves confused by the whole affair and leave their lighting to the experts, yet the principles are simple and there is every reason to get

lighting design

Interior designer Maria Duff worked on this bachelor apartment. Her aim was to create a light and welcoming space. The owner, a young businessman with internet interests, wanted a contemporary style for the apartment, which is situated on the upper floors of a large period building.

The previous look of the apartment had become very dated, with a sauna-style bathroom, bright red and white tiles in the kitchen and coats of magnolia for the walls. The owner was extremely busy, and traveled a great deal, so wanted a cleaner and more ordered design with plenty of storage and an increased feeling of spaciousness.

Structurally, some minor changes were made to improve the layout and flow of natural light in the apartment. The walls around the entrance hall were reconfigured, a door to the bedroom was repositioned, and the doorway to the living room removed to allow light to pass right through the apartment from front to back. The bathroom was slightly reconfigured to open up the kitchen, where a small breakfast area was placed alongside a window. In many of the rooms curtains were dispensed with altogether while a lightweight linen blind and curtain arrangement was added to the bedroom for necessary privacy.

The lighting plan was imaginatively arranged, with specific dimmer switches provided for lights grouped in twos or threes for flexibility, allowing the owner to create very different atmospheres within the apartment according to his mood. For the living room, halogen downlighters provide the main source of ambient light, and are complemented by the addition of two pendulum ceiling lights with glass shades that hang over the dining table. There is also a reading

light by the red leather chair, plus the gentle notes of the gas-flame fireplace.

In the bathroom three alternative light sources on three separate dimmers create a variety of effects. Recessed halogen downlighters for the ceiling are complemented by character wall lights next to the combined shaving mirror and medicine cabinet, while three heavy-duty lights along

△ **A gas-flame fire provides mellow, ambient light in the lounge.**

◁ **Hanging ceiling lights are a warm, atmospheric alternative to halogen downlighters fitted throughout.**

▷ **The entrance hallway between bedroom and lounge was reconfigured to allow an uninterrupted flow of natural light from one to the other.**

the skirting board throw another haze of light out across the rubber floor and give a sense of breadth to the room. The result is an airy and atmospheric room – with light whites and sea blues for paintwork and the mosaic tiles along with a glass shower screen – despite only having one small window with frosted glass.

Downlighters mix with inset wall lights in the bedroom, throwing arcs up towards the ceiling and increasing the sense of height. The metallic and blue notes of the lights are impactive in themselves and stand out well against the neutral color tones used throughout the apartment. In the hallway a rank of chrome downlighters on the wall have a similar impact, while again suggesting a greater sense of proportion as they illuminate the maple floor.

In the study the desk was positioned by the window to receive natural light and a character wall light was posi-

tioned nearby to add to the light provided by the halogen downlighters set into the ceiling. Pieces of designer furniture such as the Erick Jorgensen sofa and the Philippe Starck plastic Bubu stool add an extra stylistic dimension to the space and coordinate well in terms of both color and texture with the other modern and contemporary pieces chosen for the apartment. The oil paintings provide splashes of color against the restrained tonal range of the interior, with the surface interest and shades of the canvases highlighted at night by the halogen bulbs above.

Clutter is kept to a minimum and storage capacity has been thoughtfully increased by adding an airing cupboard near the bathroom, plenty of units in the kitchen and a roomy walk-in dressing room in the bedroom. This is now an easy, warm, pleasing home that provides a perfect sanctuary as the world passes by outside.

△ **A powerful wall light by the desk adds extra illumination and becomes a focus for the corner of the room.**

▷ **In the study the desk is positioned by the bare, uncovered window to make the most of the sunlight. Colors are light and reflective.**

involved in choosing the schemes that will suit not just your space but the use to which you want to put it.

One of the most important elements of any lighting plan is flexibility. With so many of today's rooms – especially in the case of areas in loft studios and other open-plan homes – being multifunctional, flexibility is now becoming a necessity. In a combined kitchen and eating area, for instance, very different sorts of lighting will be needed for preparation and dining. Cooking demands a bright, clear light with a special emphasis on highlighting work surfaces and oven and hob areas. But for entertaining, most of us would opt for a more atmospheric, subtle and recessive lighting mood.

Meeting both demands in the one room might require a mixture of recessed halogen downlighters on a dimmer switch (to create bright or tempered ambient lighting), discreet fluorescent wall- or cupboard-mounted strip lights on a separate control switch (to illuminate work surfaces), plus a separate ceiling light, perhaps, (to cast an atmospheric glow over a dining table).

Lighting can be used in a variety of different ways to determine the look of the home. Ambient lighting is the main source of artificial background light and in a contemporary space it would often be provided by recessed halogen downlighters or halogen spotlights on ceiling tracks, with hanging tungsten ceiling lights as a more conventional alternative. The advantage of recessed downlighters is that they don't interfere with the line and look of the interior, but add to the clarity and desirable simplicity of a home. Hanging ceiling lights or tracked spotlights are far less subtle, although if well designed and sympathetic to the style of the interior design they can be treated as features in themselves.

Task lighting is for specific functional areas of the home, such as kitchen work surfaces, dressing tables, bathroom shaving mirrors or study desks. The choice of source can vary from fluorescent strips to directed spotlights or halogen downlighters. But with task lighting it is necessary to think carefully about areas you feel might need extra illumination. Equally, if you find that the lighting

△ **The simple addition of plug-in lamps can both manipulate the mood of a room and add to the aesthetic.**

▷ **Halogen downlighters for the ceiling and under wall-mounted units offer background and task lighting, helped by the fluorescent strip in the stove hood.**

△ **A wall light gives
extra illumination
to a corner of a
room, including the
artwork.**

◁ **Kitchen areas
need special light-
ing treatment.
Here, natural and
artificial light
work hand in hand.**

provided is inadequate, especially for permanent working areas and sited computer terminals, do think again about getting extra lighting, otherwise you may well be straining your eyes. The simple addition of an angle-poise desk light might be enough to compensate.

Accent lighting – also known as feature lighting – is the beloved friend of architects and interior designers, effectively highlighting the form and line of a building inside and perhaps also outside. Uplighters on a dramatic curved partition wall, spotlights shining upwards beneath a steel staircase, fluorescent strips tucked along roof beams – all offer examples of accent lighting that can add an extra feeling of drama to a space. It can be constructive to think broadly in terms of drama or theater, looking at the home as a stage that has to be effectively lit both to accentuate the most important elements of the set and to help the actors move around the stage and express themselves effectively.

Display lighting is another form of accenting. Artwork and sculptural pieces may deserve extra illumination to bring out color, texture and form.

Recesses and display cupboards benefit from built-in lighting effects while display lighting from above, below or to the side can completely alter the impression of an object. Lighting frosted-glass cupboard doors from behind can have a particularly powerful impact and the same effect can be achieved with glassware or translucent ceramic pieces.

Information lighting, rather like accent touches, highlights particular design elements in the home. It has a practical purpose, too, emphasizing changes in floor level – for example – or punctuating individual steps on a stairway, perhaps helping to delineate a hallway in runway-style floor lights. Information lights can be particularly important for outside spaces – especially roof terraces and decks – that might be used in the evening or at night. Stairways, levels and borders should be clearly illuminated, and not just for safety reasons.

Lighting outside spaces, creating pools of light that accentuate the shapes of plants and highlight features such as water effects, can make a powerful impression, even when

▽ **Lighting design fits naturally into a contemporary aesthetic, as with this glass uplighter.**

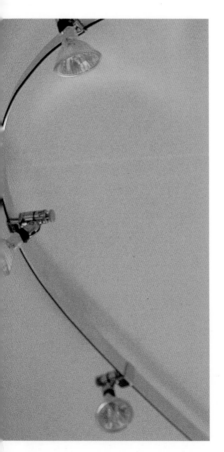

◁ **Tracked halogen
spotlights offer
great flexibility in
terms of directing
light to emphasize
areas of a room.**

viewed from the inside. Spotlights can pick out external architectural features or visually enticing shapes such as palm fronds or bamboo spindles, creating silhouettes and spanning shadows. Uplighters positioned on the ground dramatize the vertical impact of trees and branches. All these types of lighting help make any outside areas more versatile, enticing and open to use at any time.

Personal expression and individual taste come right to the fore with choices for decorative lighting. While they may have a use as task lights or even atmospheric background lighting, many table lamps and standing floor lights have an allure that lies in their sheer inventiveness. Think of Philippe Starck's horn-like Ara chrome table light, Tom Dixon's stacking Jack Light made of recycled plastic (a three-dimensional, intersecting pair of

luminous crosses) or Isamu Noguchi's sculptural series of metal and paper Akari floor lights, inspired by Japanese paper craft. These are features in themselves, self-contained design statements for the home and ripe with modernity, spliced with an element of utility.

Lighting can be used to create or encourage spatial illusions. Uplighters directed at a ceiling help give the impression of extra height in a room, with sources being either recessed into the floor, freestanding or wall-mounted. Ceiling or floor-mounted spotlights playing over side walls suggest a broader dimension to a space. In both instances, the effect is all the more effective if surfaces are reflective, shades of white being the most obvious choice. White will bounce light rather than simply soak it up, as darker colors in the spectrum might do.

Dimmer switches allow you to control these spatial effects according to the atmosphere you wish to create, alternating between openness and a greater feeling of intimacy. Most rooms will benefit from dimmer switches. Bedrooms and bathrooms, in particular, benefit from the flexibility of light levels, which allows a choice between a very clear and functional environment or a sensual, relaxing and low-key atmosphere. But remember that bathrooms, in particular, require special treatment and care and that extra rules and regulations may apply in some countries to reduce the risks inherent in any combination of electricity and water. In some regions, any main light switches will have to be outside the room, while most plug

◁ **Individual taste can be given full expression in designs for decorative lighting.**

◁ **Fiber optic lighting can be manipulated into sculptural forms; it is usually more decorative than functional.**

sockets are banned from bathrooms. Yet there are also some innovative waterproof lights that can help make the bathroom a more stirring environment – underwater lights sunken into baths, for instance, or molded into the insides of showers.

Developing technology means that remote-control lighting systems are now becoming more available, with lighting levels easily manipulated and adjusted with a miniature control wand. Movement-sensitive lighting is also making a breakthrough into the home, prompted into life the moment anyone enters a room. And new technology offers the possibility of fully computerized home lighting systems that can be programmed to suit individual needs.

m

aterials

For the loft pioneers of 1950s and 1960s Manhattan, part of the attraction of the buildings they colonized had to do with heritage. These buildings had a past, they had connotations and memories. Not so long ago they housed printing presses or carpenter's benches, sewing machines or lathes. In reality they may have been harsh environments, yet their origins were romanticized and washed down with idealized notions of honest, creative enterprise and craftsmanship. And the greatest link between the loft spaces and their commercial past lay in the materials with which they were constructed.

▷ **The natural sheen of polished granite floors contrasts with the rougher quality of the terracotta ceiling tiles.**

These were raw, semi-industrial rooms with exposed brick walls and bare wooden or concrete floors. Cables and ventilation ducts ran over walls and across ceilings. The form followed the function and these were heavy-duty utilitarian spaces. And, despite the growing design sophistication that has gradually transformed loft style as it has come of age, this raw edge still has a hold. Many loft interiors still have stretches of exposed brick, bare beams and stripped wooden floors, with the look supplemented by sleek, modern, steel work tops and industrial-style cooking ranges, rubber floors for bathrooms and concrete baths.

Yet the tendency now is to create a contrast between these raw, clean industrialized elements and the softer, more luxurious touches. By juxtaposing a hardwood floor and a suede sofa with velvet cushions, or a bare, frosted-glass window and a luxurious bed with soft linen sheets and cashmere throws, we soften and humanize our homes. We recognize the desirability and intense modernity of many industrial-style materials, but do not want to make our homes into institutions or factories, rather sensual retreats and oases of calm in the chaos of the city. It is this combination of fresh utility and stylish indulgence that informs contemporary urban style, not just for the loft but for all kinds of urban homes.

glass

Materials have the power to affect our lives, to alter the way we think. Architects and designers have always responded to new materials and ideas, but especially so through the twentieth century and into the new age, as innovation has been piled upon innovation. The entire Modernist program in architecture developed partly out of a response to new materials, as well as to existing staples that were being

◁ **Translucent glass floor panels allow light to circulate and have a clean, fresh sense of modernity.**

modified, refined and applied in new ways. These were materials that sprang from industrial processes and applications, from the machine rather than from nature. They were modern, powerful and dynamic. And architecture and design continues to develop and evolve in response to new building methods and building blocks.

One of the most influential materials in transforming the face of the urban home has to be glass. Glass may be nothing new in itself, yet the first half of the twentieth century saw the science of glass-making take architects to the point where strengthened forms could be used not just for windows and doors, but as a structural tool. Glass building blocks invented early in the twentieth century came to characterize, in part, the Art Deco era of the 1920s and 30s and are now very much back in vogue. Classic Modernist homes such as Mies van der Rohe's Farnsworth House (1951) in Illinois, Richard Neutra's Kauffman House (1947) in Palm Springs, Philip Johnson's Connecticut Glass House (1950) and

△ **Glass blends with light-colored wood and metal for a bright, modern feel.**

◁ **Glass dominates in this clean, contemporary bathroom. The white walls and reflections from the glass help increase the dimensions of the space.**

the house that Charles and Ray Eames built for themselves in California in 1949 all had vast walls of glass, with the potential for space and light maximized within these intoxicating glass pavilions.

Glass is still one of the substances we associate with the contemporary, with the new, and many architects remain fascinated by its possibilities. Think of I M Pei's glass pyramid at the Louvre, Nicholas Grimshaw's sweeping glass Eurostar terminal at London's Waterloo Station, Zeidler Roberts' Eaton Centre shopping complex in Toronto or Piers Gough's cylindrical Glass Building in Camden, North London.

Part of the original allure of loft living came from those great banks of floor-to-ceiling glass windows, which gave them a taste of industrialized modernity. Now many new-build housing projects and extensions to period homes make full use of windows, glass doors and skylights. Toughened glass floors, staircases and balconies, meanwhile, not only form vivid architectural features in themselves, but also create the possibility of making structural changes to the home without hard divisions that block the flow of light. In recent years glass has been used not just for furniture, such as glass-topped tables, but for features such as basins and baths, which have a striking sculptural beauty.

Different kinds of glass – clear, frosted, etched, painted, stained, mosaic – allow for different decorative and functional opportunities while the range of color tones adds further choice. Recent innovations like Privalite glass, which can be turned from opaque into transparent at the touch of a switch, create even greater flexibility, while new coverings for domestic glass now offer a one-way effect that allows you to see out but blocks the view of others looking in. Photosensitive glass darkens as the sunlight intensifies and clears as the sunlight weakens, just like reactive sunglasses.

Glass has become a defining medium in the home. It is the great savior of the contemporary urban space, allowing as it does so much latitude in creating interiors with an innate sense of space and light.

metallics

Metallics, like glass, have the shimmer of modernity and of "making it new." Not so much copper, bronze and iron but the alloys, the processed and plated metals: stainless steel and chrome, gleaming aluminum and zinc. The shining steel crown that caps Manhattan's Chrysler Building, designed by William van Alen, was and still is a symbol of a revolutionary architectural aesthetic. Like most skyscrapers, the Chrysler Building relies on a steel frame just to keep it in the air. For both structure and finishing, steel has helped take design onto a new and adventurous plane.

In contemporary architecture and design metallics remain iconic. Some of the most powerful structures of recent times use metal skins and design motifs, shimmering with futuristic grandeur. Daniel Libeskind's Jewish Museum in Berlin is clad with zinc; Frank Gehry's Guggenheim Museum in Bilbao is coated in titanium; Branson Coates' Museum of Popular Science in Sheffield, England, has been designed to look like four giant steel drums.

▷ **The clean lines of a limestone floor, granite work surfaces and wooden panels suggest how natural materials can be used to form a contemporary design style.**

▽ **Here the different shades and grain of wood bring both contrast and cohesion.**

◁ **A metallic spiral staircase offers a contrast to the linear design of many lofts and apartments.**

And for the inhabitants of the urban home, metallics have a similar allure. They are light and reflective, so they help distribute light through the space. They are clean, simple, functional and usually easy to maintain. There has been a trend towards adopting semi-industrial or commercial metal surfaces, cooking ranges, sinks, baths, toilets and shower units for the home and these fit in very well within contemporary interiors, especially when they contrast with softer and more natural materials.

Stainless steel, especially, has come to be a familiar note across many urban homes. Most commonly it is used for kitchen work surfaces and wall tiles, as well as for sinks. Sheet steel can easily be cut to order to fit most spaces.

Appliances once known simply as "white goods" have adapted to match. Now there is a range of steel-look refrigerators, dishwashers and laun-dry machines available to create a cohesive look.

Metallic flooring, too, is popular in the more utilitarian areas of the home such as kitchens and hallways, usually worked in studded or ribbed designs that provide a safe surface underfoot. Such floors can look really wonderful, but without underfloor heating can also be very cold and uninviting, so are seldom suited to more intimate areas such as bedrooms. Metallic-effect vinyl floor tiles are an alternative and can be warmer and a little softer to the touch. Ceramic tiles with a metal-lic look are another good option, not just to create a steel effect but in copper tones, bronze and other shades. Similarly, many new wallpaper designs experiment with metallic looks and effects.

With detailing – such as skirting boards, light switches and plug sock-ets – metallic choices are an effective alternative to more conventional

▷ **Iroko hardwood was used for the stairs in this home. It forms a strong contrast with the tubular steel and wired banisters.**

▷ **Wooden floors can seem both natural and very contemporary.**

▽ **These birch ply floors are light and airy, warmed by underfloor heating.**

designs. In each case, though, there is a safety issue, as placing electrical junctions near conductive materials needs an expert touch.

Metal is also playing a part in architectural features. In lofts, apartments and many other homes steel staircases to galleries and other storeys have removed the need for heavy and intrusive designs in stone or wood. Spiral metal staircases, or steel steps cantilevered into side walls, can be very light and subtle and do not have to disturb the flow of light or eat up large amounts of space. The same is true of balconies and safety rails, which can be made of tubular steel to avoid the use of entirely solid barriers. Partition walls and screens, too, make use of metallics, often in shaped and molded forms, to create a softer line in the home.

wood

One of the oldest and most versatile materials for the home is wood. Timber has been a basic construction material throughout the ages, yet can still be used to create the most contemporary of appearances. It is a resource that has a timeless appeal, with its wide range of color, texture and tone.

Many early lofts featured wooden floors that were either left as they were – imperfections, knocks and all – or sanded down and resealed with varnish. Wood naturally suited the space, being unobtrusive and utilitarian but also full of character and warmth. Bare wooden floorboards are still very much a part of the evolving loft-style aesthetic, with many contemporary and even more experimental homes respecting the qualities and enduring charm of timber.

Pale woods such as maple, ash and light oaks have tended to be most popular for floors, helping to reflect light. Birch and beech, too, are common light timbers for floors, work surfaces, cupboards and furniture.

In many period buildings wooden floors have been buried under layers of linoleum, carpet or floor tiles, and it is often possible to uncover, strip and polish original wooden floors to good effect. As with the early lofts, the floors do not have to be perfect and often look better with that patina of

age burnt into the boards. Sometimes brand-new wooden floors – and especially fake wood-look floor coverings – can appear just too immaculate.

Yet with hardwoods becoming very costly, and with large, open-plan spaces such as lofts potentially very expensive to cover with flooring, there are some plywoods – made of thin wooden sheets bonded together – which can also be effective.

The most important thing is to look carefully at what you are buying and to make sure the flooring is properly laid. At their worst, plywood or laminate floors can feel very flimsy, with a spring to them underfoot, something that could undermine the character of a home. As flooring is so visible, so key to the look of a room, it is a choice that deserves some extra time and consideration. Laminates will also wear more quickly than will solid wooden timbers.

If wooden floors already exist and are simply being stripped and renovated, then it will make sense to leave them laid as they are. But if new wooden floors are being laid then the direction in which they are placed can make a difference to the look of a space. Laying boards lengthways can make a room seem longer, while laying them across a room widthways can make the room appear wider than it really is. Placing boards in a diagonal pattern helps to break up the strict, regular delineation of a space. Other treatments, such as wood blocks laid like bricks or tiles, as well as traditional parquet, can also help diffuse very linear spaces.

Different varnishes and stains can be used to alter the shade of wooden floors and surfaces, although it is best to use special heavy-duty varnishes for floors. Similarly, while painting floorboards can be very effective, it is important to use specialist paints such as strong oil-based or yacht paint. Other wooden surfaces such as skirting boards, doors and window frames will usually require simple gloss or satinwood, but painted floors and stairs will, naturally, have to take a lot more punishment.

△ **Concrete floors contrast with the slatted wood panels covering an internal "river."**

▷ **A curving wall sheltering a spiral staircase – a design feature in itself.**

stone

Like wood, stone can seem both very primal and strikingly modern at one and the same time.

White Spanish limestone or black granite can seem as futuristic as the most high-tech of machine-processed materials, yet are perfectly natural. The danger of real stone, for flooring especially, is that it can seem cold and even unwelcoming, especially over a large floor area. Cost is also clearly a consideration. Yet with underfloor heating or floor-mounted convector radiators, stone can be warmed, and it can be softened with rugs and tactile furnishings.

Flooring is often treated as an afterthought, as though it is unimportant, yet in open-plan spaces especially – where flooring covers such a large and obvious area – choice of flooring can be among the most difficult of decisions. Practicality is one of the deciding factors in choosing stone for flooring and may limit your options,

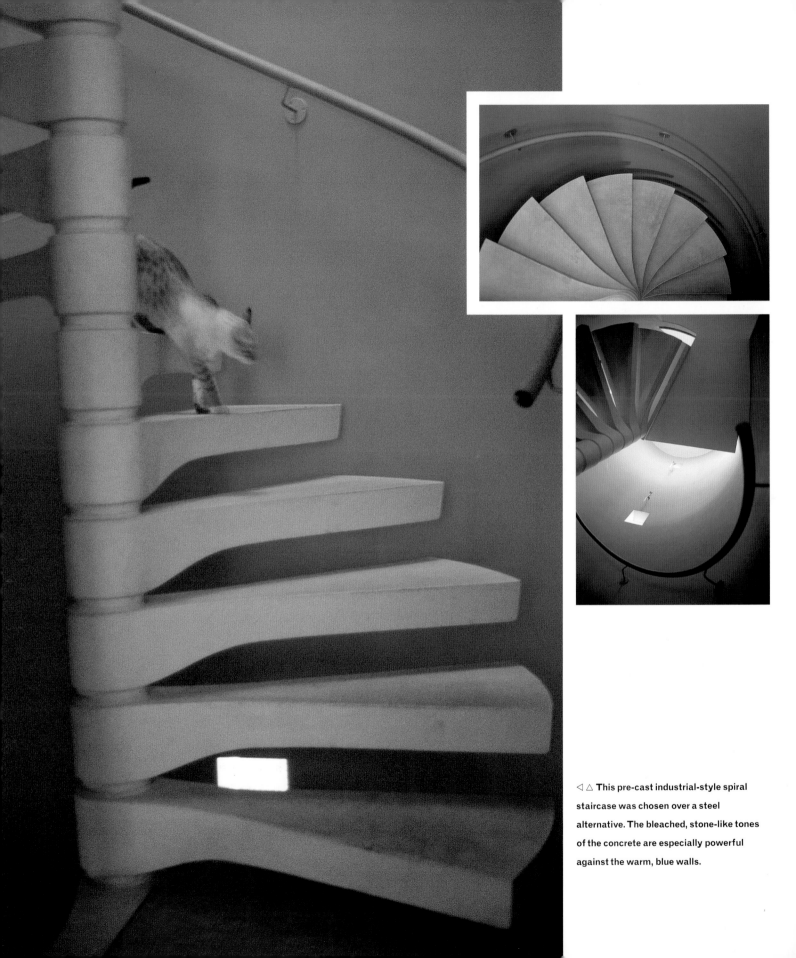

◁ △ **This pre-cast industrial-style spiral staircase was chosen over a steel alternative. The bleached, stone-like tones of the concrete are especially powerful against the warm, blue walls.**

especially in areas such as bathrooms and kitchens. Some porous stone, such as sandstone or limestone, can stain. You will need advice on whether it can be sealed and polished, and whether or not in doing so the color of the stone might be affected. The green and blue-grays of slate look beautiful as a surface, and are generally waterproof, yet slate can both stain and scratch, making it a difficult material for work surfaces and even for flooring in more utilitarian rooms.

Granite and marble are very hard-wearing, although marble in particular is sometimes regarded as ostentatious. Yet for work tops they have dramatic power and commonly find their way into kitchens and bathrooms. Used selectively they can also work very well for flooring. With marble and granite, as with many kinds of stone, there is a great deal of variation in color and pattern within the generic names given to various different types, so try to look at a sample from your supplier before committing yourself to a purchase.

Industrial materials such as terrazzo and concrete have a similar

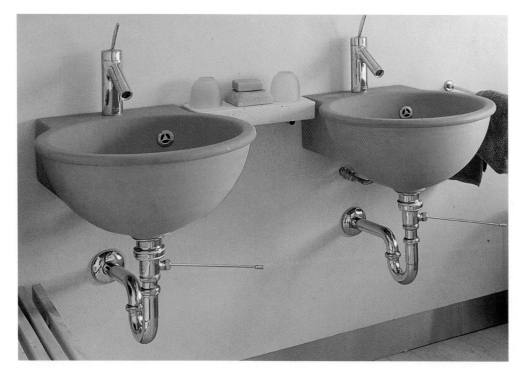

appeal to real stone. Made with an aggregate of granite or marble chips mixed with cement, terrazzo slabs have long been used in commercial spaces such as shopping centers. Now terrazzo is also being used in the home to give a clean, uncompromising and contemporary look, although it can be relatively expensive.

Concrete, however, is a different story. Like steel, concrete has changed architecture, attracting Modernists, Post-Modernists and Minimalists alike. To some critics concrete is anathema – an insult to design – that tainted the mass social housing projects of the 1960s and 70s. Yet concrete has opened up possibilities to rethink shape and form, to create more organic or sculptural buildings such as Frank Lloyd Wright's circular cathedral of art, the Guggenheim Museum in

△ **A pair of terracotta-colored ceramic sinks are enhanced with Philippe Starck– designed chrome faucets.**

New York (1959), Eero Saarinen's aero-dynamic TWA terminal at JFK Airport (1961), or Tadao Ando's Church of the Light in Osaka, Japan (1989).

The great advantage of concrete is that it can be easily poured or cast, allowing great flexibility in its use. The raw, industrial edge of concrete can be softened if it is sealed, painted, varnished or polished. Pigments can be added in to the concrete mix itself to create color tones, with purer whites especially powerful. And pouring a concrete floor creates a seamless feature, a sheet of pure white or gray, which when sealed and polished appears every bit as fine as real stone flooring.

It is, though, a hard and ungiving material, and in the home designers often consider ways of breaking up the simple monotony of a concrete surface by using different floor levels, or by creating shallow recesses in the floor where other materials such as wood or perhaps seagrass matting

▽ **Marble and granite can be sourced with a strong dapple or grain in the stone.**

▷ **A stone flagged floor brings character and a textural appeal to this kitchen.**

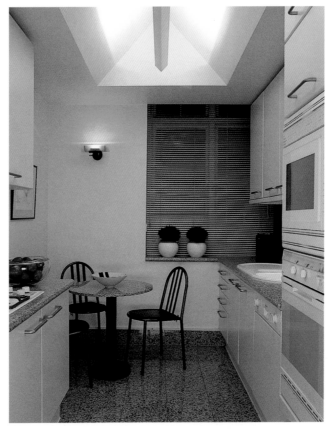

might be laid. This helps create textural contrast and a fine juxtaposition between the natural and the artificial.

Polished plaster and stucco can also have the look of stone. Moroccan-style *tadelakt*, for instance, is made with sand and quicklime and can be painted and polished to create an alluring marble-like look. It can also be molded quite easily into organic shapes and many Moroccan architects are rediscovering its properties for molded fireplaces, or baths and showers that merge seamlessly into their surroundings, as well as for walls and floors. Some paint effects, too, try to emulate the look and feel of stone, although such treatments at the more ornate end of the scale can be at odds with a restrained, simple and contemporary take on urban style. With stone or concrete you should always try to make sure the drama and impact of the material does not impinge upon the need for comfort, color and warmth in the home.

case study

the ron arad loft

This dramatic loft by architect and designer Ron Arad was created on the canvas of an empty, top-floor shell sold as part of the redevelopment of a 1950s office block. The buyer, an investment banker who had spent time in Manhattan, wanted Arad to create a open, New York-style apartment.

Arad's solution for dividing the public and private arenas of the loft was to create a twisting "hull" running right through the middle of the loft, which formed a centerpiece to the whole apartment. Part of the hull's mezzanine level is open to the main studio room, to allow light to filter over – rather like a convertible car with the roof down – and contains a secluded relaxation room and a separate study, with access to a guest bedroom to the rear. Beneath the hull shelter a dining zone and a kitchen open to the main studio, plus a long, hidden central hall with a mass of storage cupboards. The master bedroom and bathroom are at the back of the apartment.

The futuristic, curving form of the hull – made with a steel frame and laminated hardboard – was painted in gray to give it a metallic feel, which is picked up in choices for materials elsewhere in the apartment. Stainless steel has been used to coat the base of the curving breakfast bar, for window sills and porthole surrounds and for gleaming wall sections by the entrance hallway. The curving dining table, also designed by Arad, is made of steel polished to a mirror effect while the hidden stairway up to the gallery is made of metal steps.

The crisp, shimmering, semi-industrial tones of the metallics are tempered by the pale oak floors, the plywood of the Arne Jacobsen dining chairs and the rug in the corner

▷ **Pale oak floors help lighten and soften the space, while the metallic look of the painted plywood "hull" is echoed by steel fittings and metallic pieces of furniture.**

▷ **The gray suede of the armchair and sofas fits in with the color scheme and helps to provide comfort and textural contrast.**

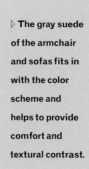

▷ The curving lines of the hull and breakfast bar help to loosen the linear quality of
the basic structure.

▷ **Metal steps lead up to the mezzanine gallery above. The stairway semi-partitions the kitchen from the main studio.**

▽ **The gleaming heavy-duty blue gloss of the kitchen units is both practical and impactive.**

◁ **An internal glass window creates a bold interface between bathroom and bedroom, allowing light to percolate between the two.**

of the main studio, which is used to delineate another relaxation zone. The gray suedes of the armchairs and sofa, cowering under the giant corner cactus, add other soft, textured touches to the design.

Whites for the walls and the pale floors make the most of the light cascading in from the banks of studio windows, complete with sliding doors to a balcony area. Splashes of color come through in the deep, shining navy blues of the recessed kitchen units – complementing the metallic grays – while the bold reds of various different Arad-designed chairs in the studio, bedroom and central hall add a rich and colorful contrast.

In the main bedroom – with its full-height ceiling and banks of storage cupboards – the most dramatic element is a plate-glass window, forming a connection with a sumptuous en-suite bathroom. Seen from the bedroom the internal window frames the bathroom like a painting, also allowing light to filter between the two rooms. It is such a clean and simple idea, yet so very effective – like the mezzanine hull – in maximizing the sense of space and light while simultaneously creating a strong visual impact.

The bathroom itself is lightly sectioned off into a wet room area containing a large jacuzzi bath, basin and chrome coil radiator. Walls and floors are tiled in small, sandy ceramic tiles. Elsewhere in the bathroom the floor is in wood, forming a natural connection with the rest of the apartment, while behind the wet room sits a private toilet area.

The design scheme for lighting in the apartment mixes recessed ceiling downlighters with hanging halogen ceiling lights and the occasional spotlight and character standing lamps, also designed by Arad. Warmth is provided by a combination of sleek vertical radiators and low, industrial-style coil heaters.

△ **Exposed brick-work possesses an uncomplicated charm when treated as an integral part of the design of the home.**

ceramics

Some ceramic tiles effectively copy stone, but tend to be cheaper and are often more practical than the originals. Ceramic, slate-look floor tiles, for example, successfully emulate the varying color tones of real slate while also being stain- and scratch-resistant, as well as very low maintenance.

Ceramic tiles have long been a staple for the home, of course, especially for kitchens and bathrooms. The choice of finishes, shapes, colors and styles continues to grow, from the rustic, mediterranean quality of terracotta tiles through the common white, shining ceramic square to painted, patterned and glazed tiles of every kind that are readily available today.

Manufacturers and their designers continue to rethink and reinvent ceramics, creating options that are very contemporary in feel, such as metallic-style ceramics, or rich mosaics in deep Oriental colors that now come in inter-connecting sheets to make them easier to lay.

At the same time, ceramic tiles are very hard-wearing and largely water-resistant, and can be used to create personalized patterns, motifs and gradations in color or texture to individual designs.

Brick, if it can be labeled a ceramic, is also very much part of the whole loft aesthetic. Old, bare brick walls create an extra layer of interest in color and texture. Panels of exposed and cleaned brick in a "frame" of surrounding plaster or tiling can look arresting, almost like an abstract piece of artwork, and can again provide a point of contrast in an otherwise sleek treatment of a space.

With any loft conversion or period home it pays to look at just what materials your building might already have in place, and which can be incorporated into the look you want to create. Perhaps discuss with an architect or designer what you might be able to make use of or uncover, such as brick walls, wooden boards or stone floors. Reusing original materials in this way usually adds to the character of the space and, if sympathetically incorporated into an interior plan, should not be at odds with any desirable sense of modernity that you may be trying to achieve.

▷ **Shining black ceramic tiles and stainless steel work tops give a stylized sanitary quality to this galley kitchen.**

▽ The vibrant
blue glaze of these
ceramic kitchen
tiles provide deep,
intense color.

▷ **Natural carpet-ing blends in perfectly with this contemporary Scandinavian style, which is rich in wood and natural colors.**

naturals

The value of texture is sometimes neglected by Minimalists and other architectural purists. Yet texture – or rather contrasting kinds of texture – is one of the great pleasures of interior design, and a valuable tool in creating a comfortable, stimulating home. A house without contrasting texture, like a house without color, can feel institutional and monotonous.

This desire for comfort and stimulation partly explains why there has been such an interest in rediscovering natural materials for flooring and matting – such as coir, seagrass, jute and sisal – that are so rich in texture. Against semi-industrial materials such as metal or concrete they have the power to soften and humanize an interior while still being in keeping

with contemporary style. These are all natural plant fibers – mostly sourced from Southeast Asia, China and India – with an ethnic appeal. Some may feel a little too prickly underfoot, some may stain and wear too easily, but all have a natural charm.

Seagrass is perhaps the smoothest and most stain-resistant of the group. Sisal is among the most versatile and, for an alternative to the neutral straw tones most familiar to us, can be dyed in alternative colors. Most of these natural fiber materials now come with rubber backing, which makes them easier to lay and more robust, and can often be found used not just as carpeting but as carpet tiles, runners or matting.

Wool can provide a softer and more comfortable alternative to these

rough, natural fibers, but with a similar texture and color range. Wool is one of the most traditional and yet also one of the most enduring of materials for flooring, again constantly updated in contemporary designs and colorways.

Burlap, raffia and other natural-look coverings – sometimes made of cotton, linen or synthetics – are being widely used as wall coverings, with powerful results in texture and tone. And leather, a material which does tend to swing in and out of fashion, is currently being explored not just for upholstery but for floors and walls, in the form of toughened tiles. The natural, neutral shades of such choices sit well with the light touch and restrained design vocabulary of loft style and open urban spaces.

◁ Sisal matting
provides texture
and natural color
tones. A recessed,
hinged wall easily
divides this
L-shaped bedroom
into two when
guests stay over.

brick, wood and metal

This loft in a former turn-of-the-century hat factory was also bought as a shell. The young, married couple who bought it – a novelist and a theater producer – turned to an architect friend. Together they created a conversion that respected the original proportions and origins of the space.

To preserve as much of the original structure as possible, complete with vaulted roof and banks of skylights, a fluid partition wall was created along one side of the loft. The gentle curve of the white wall helped to soften the hard edges of the space and lessened the shock of separating off a private bedroom, bathroom, shower room and entrance hallway. A gallery study, reached via a light metallic, spiral staircase offers another secluded room but, again, is designed so as not to intrude on the main studio, with a tubular balcony that allows light to circulate. Rush matting on the floor of the mezzanine gives a contrasting texture to the flooring in the rest of the apartment.

Respecting the original aesthetic of the building, and working with the available materials, the architect kept the exposed brick walls as they were found and painted the wooden ceiling white. Pale American–oak floorboards were laid. A kitchen was created at one end of the studio, complete with a central island holding the sink, hob, dishwasher and stove, plus a steel exhaust unit above. Cherry wood was used for the kitchen units, with a glossy black granite for the work top, which came in one piece and was so large and heavy that it had to be hoisted in through the windows by crane. The windows at the kitchen end of the space are kept bare, as there is no possibility of being overlooked in this part of the loft.

△ **The tubular spiral staircase and gallery banisters tie in with the original metal ceiling struts.**

▷ **Oak floors, painted wooden ceiling and wooden furniture create a strong natural base for the look of the loft.**

△ Leather against
brick offers
varying textures
and rich, warm
natural colors.
Artwork stands
out well against
the bare backdrop.

A relaxation zone was created at the opposite end of the room, right next to the largest set of windows. At night, light linen curtains block out the city and the views of neighboring apartment and office blocks, but are translucent enough not to block out too much daylight. A bank of bookcases to one side provides storage. A beech dining table sits in the center of the room and individual pieces of furniture, such as the multi-colored leather sofa and the brown leather armchair, help to both personalize and soften the space. The emphasis throughout is on a natural color range, but with splashes of contrasting brights from the sofa, cushions, curtains and objects such as the large blue ceramic vase. Artwork stands out against the bare brickwork, just as in many studio lofts of the 1950s and 60s SoHo bohemians.

The lines and detailing of the studio have been kept as simple as possible. There are no baseboards, for instance, while necessities such as refrigerators are neatly tucked away into recesses. Touches of greenery, encouraged by the semi-glasshouse effect provided by the skylights, have been added, with potted ivy tumbling down over the curving line of the grand partition wall.

In the bedroom the brick walls are painted white to help reflect light while in the bathroom a ceiling porthole to the mezzanine study above provides added daylight. Bedroom storage cupboards surround the entrance to the bathroom while on the opposite side of the room there is another doorway to a room for showering, with floors and walls coated in ceramic tiles.

△ **Plants and tumbling ivy spilling from the gallery above offer greenhouse touches and stand out all the more against the plain white background.**

▷ **Warm colors and soft textures for curtains, cushions and upholstery create a more sensual atmosphere in the main relaxation area of the loft.**

▽ **Despite its semi-industrial flavor, the bare brick walls and fireplace fit in well with the uncomplicated style of the loft.**

△ **An original steel and glass kitchen from the early 1970s reaches the heights of contemporary style.**

◁ **Rich cherry wood units and a black granite work surface create a sleek island kitchen, all the more dramatic for its contrast with the brick.**

kitchen materials

The two rooms in the home that are the most complicated and the most difficult to get right are the kitchen and the bathroom. Both involve a whole set of extra problems to do with water supplies, electricity and sanitation. And as the two most functional, utilitarian spaces they tend to be the areas where materials and fittings need an added level of attention.

With kitchens there has been a move towards a semi-industrial, semi-professional look, with a choice of materials such as stainless steel for work surfaces, glass or ceramics for wall tiles, and perhaps ribbed rubber, vinyl or even designer linoleum for floors. The fact that porous or easily damaged surfaces are usually impractical for kitchens means that the kitchen will usually have a different look to the rest of the home, yet without too much of a stylistic change. In lofts and other open-plan spaces, using different materials, especially for flooring, can have the positive effect of helping to zone off the kitchen from the rest of a studio space, without using any solid division.

Open kitchens especially demand good ventilation and extractors so that the space is not overwhelmed by the smell of cooking. In planning any kitchen it is important to think about how you will actually use the space, designing an ergonomic environment where surfaces are at the right height, where storage capacity clears away kitchen clutter and where inevitable spills and splashes won't ruin a floor or nearby wall.

The growth of modular kitchens is providing greater flexibility in how one organizes kitchen space, and a cheaper alternative to a fully custom-made design. Existing kitchens, meanwhile, can sometimes be effectively renovated and refreshed by redecorating units with hard-wearing paints such as oil-based, replacing cupboard handles and key fittings such as faucets, and removing outmoded flooring and wall tiles, replacing them with more contemporary equivalents.

bathroom materials

A bathroom is an area of the home that brings a wealth of practical and functional considerations, but should

▷ **An indulgent and luxurious space rich in chrome, stone and wood, and softened by bath linen and personal touches.**

also be an indulgent, sensual room where you can enjoy spending time – a point not always applicable, for many of us, to the kitchen. Creating this balance between function and comfort, especially in the choice of materials, can be challenging, but very rewarding when done successfully. No great surprise, then, that many contemporary architects and designers, such as Andreé Putman, Philippe Starck, John Pawson and Masakazu Bokura, have spent so much energy and time concentrating on the bathroom, working to achieve a combination of style, practicality and pleasure.

One of the first priorities with the bathroom is to get the basic technology absolutely right. There has to be a more than adequate supply of piping hot water on demand, together with good pressure for showers. If pressure is inadequate, look at installing pumps to boost the flow. Ventilation, insulation and heating are also important in avoiding condensation damage and in making the space warm and enticing.

Creating a wet room is one way of mixing practicality and pleasure – a bathroom that is completely watertight, with tiling or perhaps sealed and waterproofed plaster or concrete, and extra drainage through the floor to clear any water away. It is an extension and adaptation of the idea of the Turkish bath or even the sauna to a domestic arena, softening the look with color, texture and personal touches such as oils, perfumes, soaps, bath mats and bathing towels.

Alternatively, the room itself can be zoned, with a semi-enclosed, water-resistant wet zone and a more luxurious area that uses softer materials and coverings for dressing, relaxing and pampering. Between the two extremes lie many solutions using ceramics, watertight stone, glass, chrome fixtures, natural textures and also wood, which can be used not just for bathroom floors and cupboards but baths as well. Think of the traditional Japanese idea of the cedar tub, which is gaining in popularity in the West.

Allow yourself choices between bathing and showering, between quick exits and slow, relaxing experiences. Remember to create adequate storage to clear away all the flotsam in favor of simplicity, particularly if the bathroom doubles as a utility or laundry room. Bathrooms are sometimes half-heartedly sandwiched into a small, semi-redundant space. Yet they are a vital asset, a saleable commodity and a necessary indulgence, so deserve care and investment.

▷ **This cast concrete bath has a built-in heating element that helps keep the water warm during bathing.**

color

For much of its life the regulation color of the loft has been white. For the Modernists and Minimalists white was also the color of choice, so suited to reflecting light and offering pure simplicity to any contemporary space. Yet there is now a growing reaction against such a limited and limiting approach. We are learning to experiment a great deal more with paint colors again, even if the tendency is still towards paler shades and a restrained, natural touch.

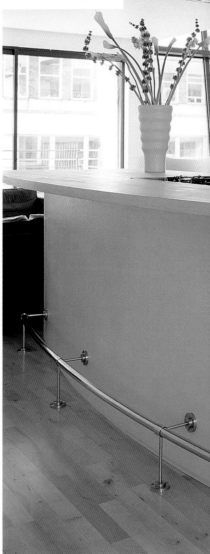

Color is tied closely to individual style, perhaps the easiest and most personal expression of taste as well as one of our most subjective decisions for the home. Color helps us to feel at ease, to feel calm and relaxed.

A child's bedroom or playroom will usually be painted in bright colors to stimulate the senses, to create a reassuring and warm environment. Yet we have tended to forget that the adult often reacts in the same way as the child, that simply trying to eliminate color in the name of style or fashion can too often result in sterile, unenticing homes without any of the pleasures of contrast, adventure and character that come from a more imaginative approach.

Today there is real recognition that use of color can instantly transform a room and sharply influence its whole atmosphere and dynamic. It may be hard to get the choices right, but if you get it wrong first time, simply repainting a wall is one of the easiest changes to be made in any home. Many architects or interior designers, after all, will paint a room several times over, in varying shades, until they feel they

have exactly the tone they are after. And color is a valuable tool in designing a home, in helping to create different atmospheres and moods, and in creating different zones within open-plan rooms. It can also affect our perceptions of space and light.

But color choices are not simply about paintwork. Color shines through in materials and furnishings, fabrics and objects – all coming together to form the many layers of color and texture that go to make up a room. It may be that a particular architectural element – the red brick of an exposed wall panel or the beach tones of a sandstone fireplace – will form a spark around which to plan the color scheme for a room. The same might be true of a favorite painting or piece of furniture. Whatever the inspiration, cohesion and harmony are the defining principles when coloring the contemporary urban home.

white

It is not difficult to see why white has such an enduring appeal for designers and architects alike, why it has become such a feature of the urban

△ **Rugs on the floor and walls of this loft provide the main splashes of color, enriched by the sunlight.**

▷ **Restrained color choices for this open-plan kitchen allow the shades and textures of materials such as the wooden and tiles floors to stand out.**

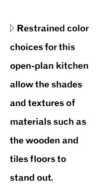

▽ **The deep blues
of the kitchen units
look fresh and
vibrant against the
black granite work
tops and lime-
stone floor.**

△ **Soft, dark velvet cushions stand out against the whites of linen and walls and add a luxurious touch to the bedroom.**

◁ **Simply varying the colors of the dining chairs adds interest to this dining zone, effortlessly taking the space beyond the monochrome.**

home. It is reflective, helping to bounce light around a room rather than soak it up, as darker colors tend to do. It is simple, helping to accentuate the line and form of a space. It is subtle, providing a neutral backdrop against which even the smallest of contrasts in texture and tone can be effective. It has a wonderful flexibility, sitting well with the most natural of finishes or the industrial precision of machine-tooled metals.

For the Modernists white was an instinctive and logical choice for both inside and outside the home, an ally in the project to create a better sense of openness and light within architecture and interior design. It allowed the sheen and subtle distinction of materials to come through: the light and airy greens of glass, the shimmer of metallics, or the warmer shades of

wood of all kinds. To some extent the Modernists were also reacting against the love of color, pattern, ornament and interior excess common to earlier architectural styles.

The availability of purer whites from around the 1920s, created by using titanium oxide, was welcomed by the Modernists, who have always been associated – sometimes unfairly – with a strict aversion to brighter tones. Even now it is a shock to be reminded that sometimes even the Modernists loved to experiment with color, as in the blue and gold mosaics in the bathroom of Le Corbusier's Villa Savoye, or the deep reds used for the window frames and woodwork in Frank Lloyd Wright's Falling Water.

For the pioneers of the loft movement, including the developers and designers who helped take lofts into

the mainstream, white was also an instinctive choice to capitalize on the luxurious sense of light and space. Lighter colors suit light space, darker colors suit more intimate and shadowy regions, so it was rational to go for white. And across the wide areas of open-plan rooms great swathes of bold, bright color could be just too much, becoming the focus of the room to the point of distracting the eye from the spatial and textural pleasure of the loft itself.

Sadly, white has all too often been treated as an escape clause, an excuse not to think about other colors, about texture and contrast. People paint their homes white without thinking, without considering whether the color is right for the space or not. Similarly, homeowners sometimes think that simply by painting a dark room white the room will be magically transformed into an airy space, and they fail to address the basic issue of promoting natural light. The result is a dark room that just happens

△ **The tones of wood, ceramics and leather – as well as the colors of artwork – stand out in this neutral context.**

▷ **Compared to the neutral tones of walls and furniture, the greens and blues of the painting become all the more powerful and the picture tends to draw the eye.**

to be painted white – another cold climate.

The way to make white work, to see white at its most effective and charismatic, is to think in terms of contrast. Even within the category of white there are a multitude of permutations, with countless shades from sandy whites, to stone, cream, vanilla, oatmeal, porcelain and bone. Using different tones of white helps move way beyond the monochrome, creating a richer and more appealing sense of variation. Woodwork, ceilings, walls, baseboards and other parts of a room can be treated in subtly different shades while a neutral white backdrop allows the texture and tint of fabrics and furnishings to stand out more effectively, creating layer upon layer of finely shifting color.

A varying white base to a space allows for experimentation with dramatic, isolated splashes of color. A single wall might be painted a brighter tone to create a feature, a centerpoint in the home, or to bring out the beauty

of architectural elements. Brighter tones within artwork stand out strongly against this neutrality while the richer colors and soft attractions of velvet cushions, suede or leather armchairs, or boldly colored floor rugs or dhurries, become all the more distinctive.

neutrals

The idea of creating an unobtrusive background, against which textural contrasts and variations in materials and furnishings shine through, carries over into the neutral color palette:

△ **A calm cohesion comes of mixing neutrals and whites, while the green of palm fronds becomes vibrant in juxtaposition.**

▷ **The subtle, natural tones of furniture and paintings shine against white-painted walls, creating strong interest within a very restrained use of color.**

straw yellows, golden browns, biscuit colors, fawn, stoney or metallic grays, pale blues and a hundred variations on the theme. These are unassuming, inconspicuous choices, yet they can have a subtle but important effect within the home, especially in bright, open-plan spaces where even slight variations in tone and textural emphasis can seem striking under the gaze of sunlight. Spot coloring with a vase of flowers, a richly colored throw, or an accent in upholstery can be very powerful in such a neutral context and quickly helps take a space beyond the ordinary.

By their very nature neutrals have the flexibility to sit with most other colors, to mix with all kinds of materials and fabrics. They are calming, peaceful and can be much warmer than whites. Gray is regarded alongside white as a key transition color that acts as an effective border between areas that might otherwise clash. For this reason it is often used for hallways or landings where rooms in many colors might interconnect.

Yet even within this subdued color palette the potential for altering

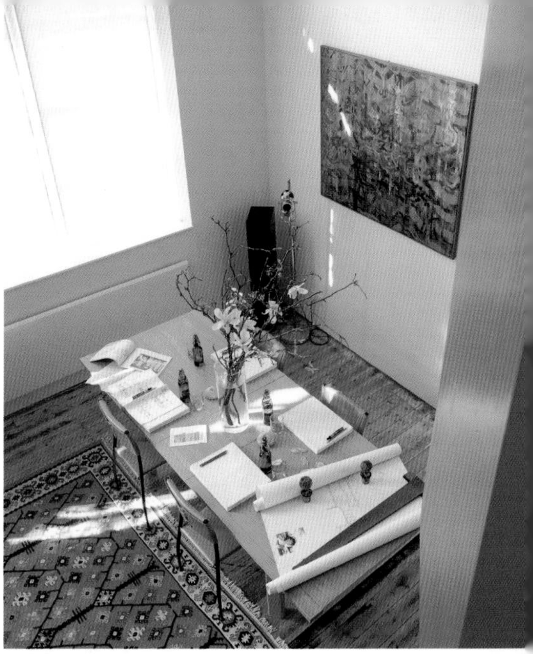

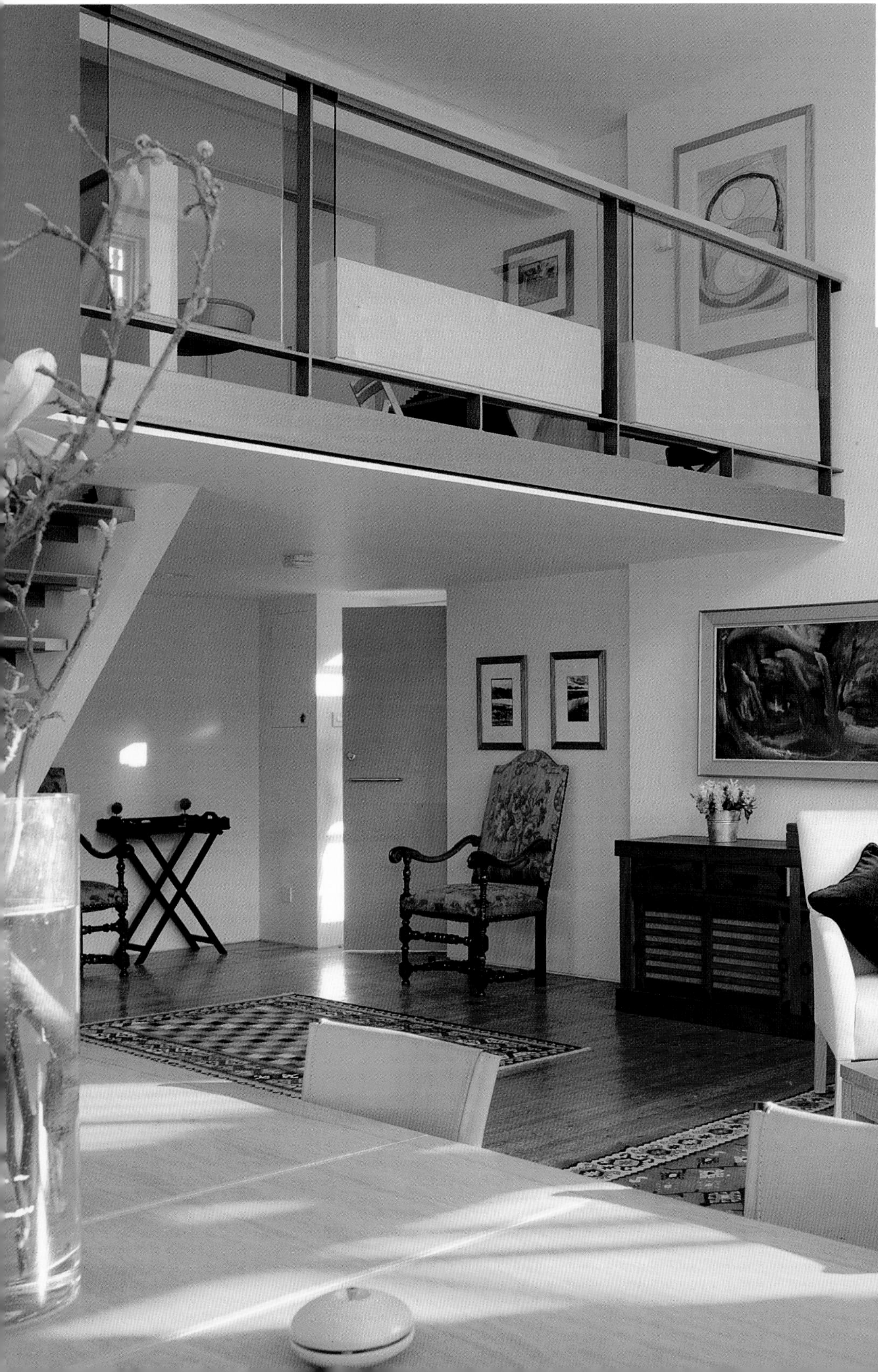

bold and bright

Interior designer Christina Fallah created this fresh loft look for a young, professional couple within the redevelopment of a old school. The public and private areas were separated with a mezzanine gallery holding a study, bedroom and one of the apartment's two bathrooms.

◁ **The red of the curving wall concealing the mezzanine transforms the apartment, adding warmth and drama.**

◁ **White predominates for walls, allowing splashes of red in paint work, carpets and fabrics to appear dynamic.**

The majority of the wall space was painted off-white to maximize the light pouring in from the large windows – most of which were kept bare or semi-screened with translucent linen blinds – and to help tie the whole apartment together. For visual impact and a sense of warmth, a glossy red was used to paint the curving solid wall area of the gallery, making it stand out all the more against the neutral backdrop. The eye is instantly drawn to this flash of red, which highlights the dominant architectural element in the apartment. The same color was also used for the internal stairway that runs from the studio room up to the mezzanine.

Red and white became the dominant colors throughout in this apartment. In the main seating area white was also used in the upholstery for the sofa – originally bought in turquoise – and for the matching armchair. In the main studio the reds are picked up in the pattern of the large kilim laid over the reclaimed oak floor, in velvet cushions and dried flowers, and in the recessed panels of exposed red brick that look all the more effective because of the way in which they contrast with the smoothly plastered white walls that surround them. Both floors and brickwork serve as reminders of the building's heritage, as well as offering opportunities to add character to the space. Even the subtle pinks and lilacs of spring blossoms stand out within the considered, judicious scheme.

The warm, natural tones of the ash units in the kitchen – topped with granite surfaces plus stainless steel wall tiles – fit well with the red color notes and are echoed by the dining and coffee tables, as well as by the soft leather used for the iron-framed dining chairs. An eclectic collection of modern art becomes all the more potent against the neutral walls. Elsewhere in the apartment a vast, three-meter-long side cabinet in Chinese style houses cutlery, dinner plates and stereo while a pair of sixteenth-century armchairs by the front door is effectively juxtaposed with the contemporary style of the rest of the apartment.

◁ **Red has also been used for the stairway to the mezzanine, marking a transition from public to private space.**

▷ **The red of the gallery wall is echoed by the traditional patterned rug, which is just simple enough in its geometric design to fit in with a contemporary aesthetic.**

▽ **Natural weave matting softens the bedroom. Natural tones – including the ash wood bed – throughout make this an airy room but also a calming and relaxing one.**

△ In the gallery study a kilim adds extra warmth, helping to create the impression of a more intimate and comfortable working environment.

Upstairs, within the mezzanine, natural weave matting and a second kilim add soft, textural appeal against the smooth walls and the glass, steel and wood used for the study balcony. Items such as the roll-top desk and wooden bookcases are intended to echo the building's original function while Oriental antiques such as a recliner and campaign stool mix with the contemporary furniture. Within the bedroom, the bed itself is made of ash while storage cupboards have been built into the room to keep surface mess to a minimum. In the bathroom white ceramic tiles line the walls while green towels on sea-green shelving add another colorway.

The apartment shows how loft-style living has moved well beyond Minimalism to a more comfortable and individual approach, yet with a simple cohesion in color and pattern. Old mixes with new, antiques with the contemporary, yet the apartment comes together naturally and seamlessly. The whole apartment was also decorated top to bottom in just eight weeks, suggesting that creating a stylish, comfortable home does not have to consume every inch of one's being for months upon end.

 **Sandy velvet grays add a sumptuous, earthy touch to a simply decorated and uncluttered bedroom.**

perceptions of a space can be compelling. Painting a ceiling a shade or two lighter than the rest of the room accentuates height, which explains why most ceilings tend to be white. Within a long, thin room painting the side walls in a pale color, with a darker shade for the far walls at either end can give the impression of greater width and a clearer sense of proportion. Modest color changes can help create a zone within an open-plan room. Warmer tones for wall sections next to an area for relaxing or eating work well in engineering a tranquil atmosphere.

earth

While studio spaces and public rooms will suit lighter colors, parts of the home such as bedrooms and bathrooms often deserve a more intimate, hedonistic treatment. These are the private parts of the home, where it is important to feel relaxed, comfortable and easy, to feel protected and secure. Here, it can be better to opt for a more personal choice of colors, which provoke an emotional, sensual reaction.

Rich, opulent, earthy colors such as deep chocolate browns, ruby reds,

crimson, mahogany and vermilion might suit these most individual of spaces, providing a warm and womb-like effect. They are colors that provide a sense of enclosure, making intimidating spaces more welcoming. Again, these are colors that are natural, but also indulgent and luxurious. They sit well with deep woods, such as iroko or teak, and with soft, tactile fabrics such as cashmere, fake furs and real wool for bedding and furnishings. Leather and suede, too, fit wonderfully well into the mix.

Mediterranean colors such as terracotta, sunshine yellows and sea tones offer a slightly more rustic and lighter alternative to the richest of earth tones, along with Moroccan-style indigo blues. They can suit bathrooms, in particular, where it is always hard to strike that balance between rich indulgence and a lighter appeal.

When choosing any color, remember that color chart tones generally look darker when the paint is spread over larger areas, so pick extra testers

◁ **Deep blue walls in this bedroom, tied to the tones of the bedspread, help create a seductive, enticing retreat.**

▽ **The color and rich texture of leather glows in sunlight against the unobtrusive tones of wall and floors.**

that edge a few shades lighter along the color spectrum. Try painting a decent area in the room in question to see the effect and look at the color at different times of the day, as well as under natural and artificial light. Mistakes can be easily rectified, so don't be dissuaded from repainting, as color is one of the cheapest yet also one of the most important elements in the look of the home.

Be sure to consider texture within color treatments, especially in more secluded parts of the home, which deserve a tactile approach. Instead of standard emulsion look of gloss or eggshell for walls to create a vibrant and polished finish, or consider alternative strips of gloss and emulsion. Try fabric wallpapers in earthy tones, perhaps, or traditional wallpapers in linear or geometric designs that have a suitably contemporary feel.

rainbow

Although the urban home is breaking away from the restricted attitude to color promoted by the Minimalists of the 1990s, we still have a great deal to learn about using and experimenting

△ **Bright, rainbow colors in furniture and rugs form a strong palette for decorating a room beyond the shades in a paint can.**

◁ **This combination of creams and a range of beach browns creates a harmonious scheme, with the black lacquered piano dominant and dramatic.**

with color. There is still a fear surrounding the use of bolder colors in the home, a feeling that it is too extreme, too individual. There are worries about making mistakes, even though errors with paint color are so easily rectified. There is a feeling that once a color has been chosen for a room, then that's it, that's the way it must stay indefinitely. The result of all this can so often be blandness.

Part of the problem is the misguided notion that every wall in a room has to be one and the same color, that a space has to be totally uniform. But if simplicity and restraint are virtues in interior design, uniformity is not. It can be more helpful to think of walls one at a time, to consider picking out one section of a room in a brighter color, such as a bank of red in a room otherwise dominated by white. Without in any way overpowering relatively small areas, the red might provide a keynote to help theme furnishings with peri-

odic splashes of crimson and scarlet, so creating a feeling of harmony within the room.

In an otherwise neutral scheme, these splashes or banks of color stand out all the more. Brighter colors might be used across a zone such as a kitchen, both to help differentiate it from the rest of an open-plan room and to create a focus to be picked up on with accent notes in fabrics, glassware or artwork. Cupboard doors or architectural elements such as staircases or fire surrounds can sometimes be picked out in these more vibrant colors. Even painting a shelved alcove or a small recess in a brighter color than its surroundings can be enough to create a more lively, provocative design.

Rainbow colors across the spectrum are now finding their way into the urban home, usually within this kind of subtle, considered approach and the impact of even small areas of primary

△ **The colors of the headboard tie in with the lilac, creating a soft and calming space without excess.**

▷ **Not every wall in a room has to be a uniform color. Here a lilac treatment on just one wall, by the bed, is enough to lift the whole bedroom.**

▽ **Bamboo shoots and sea-green frosted glass are sympathetic with the lilac and blue beyond.**

▽ **Walls and cup-
boards don't have
to be uniform in
color. Variation
adds warmth and
theater.**

▷ **Kitchen units
painted in a
spectrum of pop
colors – spots of
color in a calm sea
of white.**

colors (red, green and blue) can be dramatic. The pop colors of the 1960s and 70s have a childlike appeal and are experiencing a resurgence – lavenders, pinks, pea greens, pistachio and acid yellows.

Yet while experimenting with color does create a greater sense of vitality and animation in the home, in contemporary urban homes, where the concentration is on light and space, on sophisticated simplicity, it can be a mistake to create too much of a mélange of bright color. To avoid creating a confused, irregular style it pays to limit the number of colors in the palette and concentrate on aiming for harmony and cohesion. Color is the greatest unifying force in design, binding together a wealth of textures and materials. By the same token, excess in pattern and color can be disruptive and destroy the calm, relaxing environment that is so important to city living, where the ability to escape pressure and stress is fundamental.

balancing color

This period home, once an old stable block, was completely reconfigured by its owners — a metropolitan businessman and his wife. Working with their architects, they rebuilt the top floor as an open-plan living and dining room, while bedrooms and bathrooms were moved downstairs.

Reconfiguring the house – which was in a poor condition before work began – turned a dark, claustrophobic area with a warren of small rooms into an airy, contemporary space full of natural light. Restyling the top floor presented an opportunity to create a small roof terrace, complete with a skylight down to the main bedroom and a porthole to the bathroom. French doors in the main studio, leading to a little balcony at the front of the house, helped maximize light in the dining area while extra skylights to the main roof helped raise light levels even further. A traditional staircase between the two floors was replaced with a light, curving steel and maple design that allows light to percolate through the hallway and has the look of a gangway to an ocean liner.

In terms of color, the studio was painted in the main with shades of white emulsion to help reflect light and reinforce the feeling of openness. Linen curtains in vanilla tones were chosen for the window and for one of the two sofas. The reclaimed maple floors that once formed the surface of an old squash court, and the limestone edging by the fireplace, reinforce the basic neutrality of the scheme, which allows the sea-glass colors of the coffee table and the frosted surface of another nearby corner table to stand out all the more. A black leather sofa creates a contrast in texture and color, echoed in the dark woods of the mantelpiece and ethnic pieces such as a stool and carved figurine. Red cushions and a vase of crimson flowers stand out to powerful effect within the restrained context, yet instantly help to warm and humanize the space.

At the other end of the studio the many colors of a Damien Hirst painting shine through against the white background while six dining chairs, upholstered in green to blue, sit around the dining table. The blue notes complement the dramatic, navy blues of the kitchen, which stands to one

▷ **The rainbow colors of the artwork and the blue-greens of the upholstered dining chairs invigorate the dining area.**

△ White for many
of the walls helps
tie the different
parts of the house
together, upstairs
and downstairs.

◁ A simple pair of
crimson cushions
seems to add heat
and brightness
against the neutral
and earthy tones
of much of the
living room.

△ **White mosaic tiles for the shower look clean and crisp.**

▷ **Light was the priority here, with wooden headboard and pieces of art on the shelves prominent against the reflective whites and creams.**

◁ **The checker board black marble and white limestone floor helps break the uniformity. With porthole and gantry-like stairway, the hall has echoes of a ship.**

side of the main studio. Cupboard units are painted this deep, rich, matt blue while maple shelving, a professional chef's range, and steel elements such as the exhaust unit and door handles reinforce the clean, contemporary style of the design. Black granite is used for work surfaces, including the smart island unit that features a balanced counter of sleek stone. Limestone is used for the floors, its light color in sympathy with the inter-connecting maple used in the main studio.

Downstairs in the hallway a black and white checkerboard effect in black marble and limestone dominates while

walls throughout much of the downstairs are painted white to connect naturally with the rest of the house.

The main bedroom features a skylight complete with blinds that automatically open up in the morning while the off-whites of the wool carpet and crisp bed linen stand in strong contrast to the rich, dark wood tones of the bed headboard. The doors front a bank of built-in cupboards. An en-suite bathroom features a curving, organically shaped shower unit complete with Philippe Starck fittings, and a white ceramic mosaic is used to coat the walls of the wet areas.

△ **These painted horizontal stripes add contrast and accentuate the width of the room.**

paints

The choice of paint colors available today has reached a point where almost anything is possible. If you still feel restricted by the choice, however, you can always mix colors yourself. There are also many choices in the type of paints available – these are broadly divided into water based and oil based.

Matt emulsion is the most common water-based paint, although traditional, soft distemper still has some currency and gives a chalky texture, as does limewash. Emulsion is the usual choice for standard walls and can help to diffuse a space, to soften dimensions, as it creates a gentle and relatively supple surface.

Emulsion does not suit heavy-duty surfaces liable to knocks, however, such as floorboards and doors, or areas such as kitchens and bathrooms, where spills may cause staining and discoloration. Varnish can be used to protect water-based paints if used on woodwork, such as floor-boards, but may affect the original hue of the colors.

Oil-based paints include standard gloss and traditional matt eggshell, as well as other mid-sheen finishes such as satinwood. Oil-based paints are tougher and more hard-wearing than water-based paints, and generally washable, making them suitable for bathrooms or kitchens. They are an obvious choice for wooden surfaces such as windows and doors, but will highlight imperfections in surfaces. Gloss surfaces have a shine to them that forms a visible and reflective barrier.

It can be interesting to experiment with various different types of paint and use them in ways which create obvious contrast. For example you could alternate gloss and emulsion on wall sections or perhaps accentuate the texture of an imperfectly plastered wall with eggshell or varnish. With any painted surface, as with color, it is important to move beyond uniform perfection, to experiment with different textures and finishes to create layers of interest.

Specialist paints are available for floors. You might look at using yacht deck paints, which mostly come in gloss finishes. For a more subtle matt finish it may be best to stain the wood, or use a suitable emulsion or eggshell, and then varnish. Other specialist paints include metallics, textured masonry paint, toughened waterproof paints for use around shower areas or baths, and paints to be used to re-coat ceramic tiles. Many surfaces, especially woodwork and bare unsealed plaster, will need priming.

◁ **These concrete panels have an irregular patina of light terracotta and cream.**

styling

The key to styling urban spaces is balance. Balance between personal treasures and a cohesive, clear and contemporary home style. With our choice in furniture, fabrics and a hundred other details we stamp our personality upon a room, we make it ours. We surround ourselves with books, pictures and scraps from our travels through geography and time – pieces with associations and memories that remind us who we are and make us feel at home.

There is always a risk in succumbing to the temptation to crowd a room with anything that catches the eye, that might just fit into the mix. Having concentrated on creating an open, light and desirable contemporary space, we wake up one day and find it suddenly crowded and cramped. This is why balance is so important – striking a happy medium between a clean, restrained look that allows strengths in the architecture and basic design of a home to shine through and the desire to have around us the things that mean the most, things that give us real satisfaction and make our lives more enjoyable.

It can be hard to limit oneself. Anyone with an interest in design tends to be a collector, a hoarder. We tend to move from one home to another and take everything with us. One way or another we inherit furniture, china and artwork, and it can be hard to admit that what has suited us well in the past just isn't right anymore. Seen objectively, this habit of transposing possessions and furniture wholesale from one space to another is not that sensible, if it is not born of

necessity. It is an outmoded approach. What suits one home or one way of living will not necessarily suit another. A loft filled with antique furniture, for instance, generally looks absurd – these delicate, ornate pieces are simply dwarfed by the proportions of the space.

The way a contemporary, modern home is furnished and styled should be in keeping with the look and feel of the space itself, taking into account scale, color, materials and texture. When furniture is chosen with the space very much in mind the look will be all the more cohesive and effective – an obvious principle of interior design, but all too easily forgotten. Sometimes it pays to keep only the most essential of treasures and start again. Built-in furniture and storage room can help to simplify the design, providing a home for much of the detritus of everyday living. Elsewhere, it can be both an indulgence and a requirement to search for styling and furnishing choices that are in keeping with the essential aesthetic of the space, where the emphasis is on preserving openness and light.

▷ **An uncluttered, cohesive interior can and should be comfortable. Here a rich, red leather armchair warms by the fireside, an ideal focus for relaxation.**

△ Innovative lighting design blends dramatically with an open staircase.

furniture

In some ways we are looking back in order to take urban home style forwards. We are looking to the example of the Modernists, and trying to build upon it and adapt or reinvent their approach. The furniture designed by the Modernist icons was created in sympathy with a complicated set of architectural priorities to do with a more open-plan way of living. The Modernists used furniture that made the most of new, semi-industrial materials and processes. Designers such as Le Corbusier, Ludwig Mies van der Rohe, Arne Jacobsen, Walter Gropius, Marcel Breuer and Alvar Aalto crossed the boundaries between furniture design and architectural work with ease and regularity, the two sides of the coin forming a part of the same aesthetic currency.

The furniture, like the architecture, played with raw and reflective materials such as tubular steel, glass and light plywood. There were Jacobsen's plywood Ant and Series 7 chairs, Mies van der Rohe's Barcelona chair in shining steel and leather and Marcel Breuer's Wassily armchair in similar

materials. And there was Le Corbusier's Basculent and Grand Confort chairs, along with his hide and steel recliners. These were pieces with a sculptural beauty; classics born of an era that stretched from the 1920s to the 1950s. Charles and Ray Eames, George Nelson and Verner Panton were also pioneers of the time. It was work that combined simplicity in form and function with true artistry and craft, with a sculptor's touch. They were and are contemporary and modern, yet also form twentieth-century classics.

Perhaps it is because the priorities of these designers and architects are so in tune with the concerns of contemporary design, the priorities and aesthetic of open living, that these designs still seem so current and relevant. Perhaps they were simply well-designed objects. Either way, many pieces by the Modernist icons are being reissued and repackaged while the originals are collector's items and in constant demand. You can buy work by Panton, Pierre Paulin and Robin Day in main-street stores and source Eames and Mies van der Rohe on the

△ **The color, texture and shape of contemporary furniture all add to the layers of interest in the home.**

◁ **This L-shaped**
sofa creates its
own comfort zone –
also delineated by
a rug over the
uniform wooden
floor – within an
open studio.

▽ **Modern furniture**
designers explore
many of the
same materials
as architects,
such as glass and
metallics.

◁ **The contrast between the linear, black leather sofa and the white, low-slung circular marble table makes for a perfect combination, pleasing in its precision.**

◁ **Positioning furniture on a paper floor plan helped the designer of this apartment coordinate furniture and divide the main room into areas for dining and sitting.**

Internet. Classic Modernist furniture is no longer the preserve of specialists and design connoisseurs, but is edging further and further into the mainstream. These pieces are common sites in today's lofts and open-plan contemporary homes.

At the same time, the design legacy bequeathed by the Modernists is being revisited and remodeled by contemporary designers such as Philippe Starck, Tom Dixon, Ron Arad, Michael Graves and Nigel Coates. As with the Modernists, these designers are creating work with a sculptural, artistic quality that needs space to be appre-

ciated, to be seen, and must not be crammed in a corner. With materials and finishes they experiment with plastics, molded metals, laminates and veneers. Their work needs a particular context and the best context is the open-plan environment of the urban home.

The Manhattan designer loft style of the 1980s developed its own set of clichés. There was the gleaming bicycle hanging from the wall, the American 1950s-style refrigerator, the chrome trash cans and the Keith Haring print. Now we have moved beyond the clichés and are intent on

creating a more individual approach, experimenting with styles and ideas in our own way. We look for pieces that tell their own story.

Whatever your particular choice, furniture should be selected to be in sympathy with the room in which it is going to be set, with an eye on color, texture and scale. A loft-style studio will obviously demand a very different approach to a small and intimate dining room. Light, open-plan spaces offer a real freedom to create a personal drama, a piece of theater, with furniture and styling, and furniture can also be used as tools in creating different zones for relaxing, dining and working. Flexibility is another issue and partly explains the resurgence of matching modular furniture that can be repositioned at will in various different formations.

Experiment with positioning furniture, without being trapped into a traditionally Western pattern of taking everything to the side of the room and leaving a wasteland in the middle. In an open-plan environment, especially, this can be counter-productive. Try drawing floor plans if necessary – as many interior designers do – to help you see how a space might be treated and then position pieces accordingly. Avoid cramping furniture together too tightly. If a piece is clearly wrong for the space then try to reconcile yourself to taking it back or sending it on elsewhere rather than hoping that one day it will magically have become everything you hoped it would. If you have real difficulty finding what you are after, consider having something made especially to your own design or brief, as this can sometimes be a cheaper way of doing things than buying designer-ware off the shelf.

Any home needs a fair degree of contrast to raise it above monotony. Choose one or two oversized pieces of furniture – a sofa or an armchair perhaps – to play with contrasts in scale. Look at subtle changes in color and texture, using leather, suede, chrome and other materials. Drop one or two older, character pieces or junk-shop finds among the layers of a room, such as a Chinese dowry cabinet or an old desk used as a dining table – objects that go beyond their original design function but that are rich in substance and virtue. Furniture taken out of its intended context, such as well-made garden or office furniture, can have great appeal within the home. Don't forget comfort, and remember that furniture should not only look right and fit in with the look of the home, but should have a function, too, and be ergonomically and physically suited to you and your purposes.

For added flexibility dining tables and other furniture can be easily mounted onto small castors for easy movement in and out of position in a open-plan area. Built-in furniture can be a great help in creating a cohesive

△ This open-plan home is rich in contrasts. Exposed brick contrasts with smooth, white walls, rich velvets and suede with pale wooden floors.

◁ Symmetry calms the eye and the mind. Here bedside tables, cushions and vases all have a twin. Only the glass-fronted cupboard breaks the spell.

▷ **Neat banks of built-in storage units hide away clothes and shoes in this dressing area, which is given a luxurious, indulgent turn with the addition of an armchair and full-length mirror.**

style while allowing more room for yourself and your other possessions to breathe. Fold-down beds, recessed desks and study areas, fold-out dining surfaces or breakfast bars – all create more flexibility in how space is utilized.

storage

One of the hidden foundation stones of contemporary urban style is storage. Minimalist architects and designers such as John Pawson, Claudio Silvestrin and Tadao Ando have relied upon vast banks of storage capacity to give them the freedom to play with clean, dramatic lines and unhindered rooms within domestic living space. Even though the tendency is now towards a more humanized and sensual approach to design, where we indulge elements of luxury and personal expression, storage is still key in creating uncluttered, open homes.

Within any home, especially a family home, there will be an enormous amount of clothing, books, china, glass, toys, papers and accounts, as well as computers, televisions, music equipment and laundry machines. There may well also be excess pieces

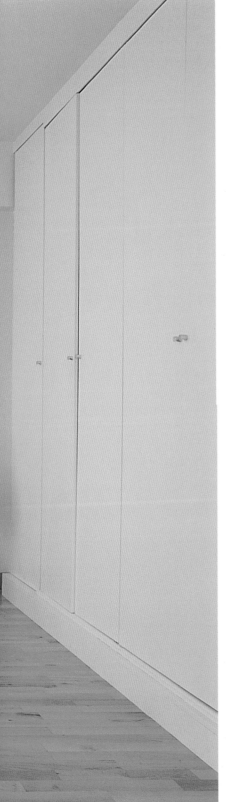

◁ **Shelving can be both functional and decorative. Here built-in shelving holds favorite pieces for display.**

◁ **These storage cupboards were cheaply made with a second-hand shop display unit, repainted with a new top added.**

of furniture, artwork and objects that need to be stored away. Walk into a house where there is inadequate provision for hiding away all this clutter and the visual chaos is obvious, resulting in stress, disorder and even discomfort.

Built-in storage is the most obvious solution. In planning or replanning a space make provision for storage with integrated cupboards and shelving, especially for functional rooms such as kitchens and bathrooms. It is best to edge towards over-capacity rather than under, as the extra leeway usually proves invaluable. Look at making the most of completely redundant spaces in the home – perhaps under stairs or within recesses and attic areas, or even within the floor – without compromising on aesthetics.

Well-designed storage units can be architectural or design features in themselves, adding significantly to the look and feel of a room and making use of fine materials, surfaces and textures such as rich woods, veneers and glass.

Storage can equate with luxury if you have the space for dressing rooms, walk-in wardrobes or utility rooms. If there is a study or work area in the home, then try to create as much storage as possible within it and surrounding it, because it is important that work does not spill over into areas that are designed for escape.

As well as built-in storage, there are many options available for freestanding units and modular shelving systems, which can also add to the look of the home. Some of these units can be used, like other pieces of furniture, to help zone an open-plan room and create a impermanent boundary around a particular area. Mobile trolleys for televisions or stereos can be quickly wheeled in and out of position to suit and cleared away when you are entertaining.

◁ **A glass shelf with modest touches such as colored towels and flowers are sufficient to raise this bathroom above the functional.**

△ **Glassware is shown off to its best effect with this custom-made shelving drawn away from the wall to allow light to pass through the translucent vases.**

◁ **Books add character to a room and should not necessarily be locked away. Here a dining area doubles as a library with a generous bank of ordered shelves.**

◁ An intimate second sitting area is tucked away on a lower level, with soft armchairs and sofa.

▽ Warm earthy suedes, velvets and cords soften and calm the hard lines of the studio space.

natural luxury

Home to a cosmopolitan young restaurant designer well used to treating spaces as individual entities, this apartment was created in a warehouse space around the back of a 1970s office block. The entire block has been redeveloped as apartments, with this being one of the most spacious.

When she moved into this loft-style apartment from a modest period home the owner had to start from scratch. Her philosophy was to bargain hunt for designer furniture and mix in cheaper pieces with a good design edge, pieces intended for this apartment alone and considered as having a relatively short life span. Almost every piece was introduced with the space in mind. Being a designer herself, the owner created her own furniture in custom-made fashion.

Separate zones in the apartment for sleeping, eating and relaxing have been neatly created by using different floor levels, without compromising on the basic luxury of the vast open space of the loft. In the main studio area furniture alone has been used to create a relaxation zone, with sofa, ottomans, coffee tables and a character leather armchair all positioned in a loose square formation close to the television set.

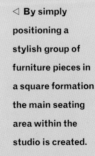

◁ **By simply positioning a stylish group of furniture pieces in a square formation the main seating area within the studio is created.**

▷ **A small study area is hidden away to one side of the low-level sitting area, so as not to be intrusive.**

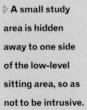

▷ **Clever storage helps keep the apartment clean and ordered. Hanging curtains hide clothes rails and shoes while screens clear away other bedroom clutter.**

The browns and whites of the furniture are in sympathy with the neutrality of the colors used on the walls, the ceiling and in the exposed brickwork. They also stand out against the pale wooden floor. The use of suedes for the ottomans and the addition of a cashmere throw, with piled cushions in velvet and cord, help soften and feminize the look while also creating a more sumptuous element within the zone. The wall mirror and Noguchi-like sculptural light in the corner help temper the area. At the other end of the studio, by a set of French windows, a reading area has been created with shelving units and a leather and steel recliner that has the feel of a classic Le Corbusier.

To the side of the main studio, two floor levels have been created one on top of the other, but without using any solid walls, so maximizing the sense of light and space. On the lowest level there is a second, more intimate living area with a soft, mellow sofa and armchairs upholstered in warm velvets. A work desk has been positioned to one side, partly concealed by a pillar. There is a separate dining area with an impactive, custom-made steel and wood table and matching chairs. The kitchen is tucked away neatly in a semi-recessed area.

The upper level forms a sleeping gallery with a steel and wire treatment for the perimeter balcony and stairway that allows light to filter through and offers no real interruption to the basic proportions of the apartment. The bed is custom-made, with purple cushions for a splash of color. The Japanese-style screens conceal a make-up area while clothes rails are screened by a set of light linen curtains, keeping the bedroom as free of clutter as possible and reinforcing the calming nature of the space.

There are few side windows in the apartment, but the sequence of large skylights provides good natural sunlight and prevents the space from feeling claustrophobic. Recessed halogen downlighters provide workhorse lighting, with wall lights and lamps in tungsten offering a more ambient and atmospheric alternative. In the one clearly partitioned room in the apartment – the bathroom to the side of the bedroom gallery – internal windows using glass bricks introduce at least some element of natural light.

△ **Different levels create zones for eating, sleeping and relaxing. Only the bathroom is hidden away.**

▷ **Despite preserving semi-industrial elements such as exposed brick, comfort comes through in styling.**

▷ **Soft sofas and recliners maximize comfort, as well as offer fine contrasts with simpler surfaces such as wooden floors.**

Shelving can also be used for display. Books, for instance, can have a decorative power. Glassware or ceramics can be set out on shelving in alcoves or recesses and become a focus when illuminated. Collections of this kind can in fact be the centerpoint around which the whole look of a room is created.

fabrics

Within loft style and the general move towards open-plan, contemporary spaces there is a tendency towards a common sense of restraint with regard to fabric, especially in the use of pattern. This restraint is partly bound up with the issue of maximizing light, so dispensing with heavy curtains in favor of bare windows or translucent treatments. It is also tied to the love of simplicity and order within open-plan living and to a belief

△ **Banks of luxurious cushions, comfortable bed covers and soft textures underfoot make this neutral bedroom an indulgent escape.**

◁ **Stone floors and clean lines are softened by the warm upholstery and rugs. Clothing hung like artwork adds unexpected texture and appeal.**

that using excess pattern can be overwhelming and obtrusive, just too complicated and domineering for the clean design aesthetic of the loft and its cousins.

But that is not to deny that fabrics have an important part to play in the look of the home. Fabrics for upholstery, window treatments and added touches such as cushions and bed throws help to soften the harder edges of a room. They are an essential ingredient in layering the design of a room, providing elements of texture, contrast and color while helping to reinforce the message of comfort, escapism and luxury that should be a part of urban living.

Tactile coverings such as suede, velvet and cord, as well as leather, are texturally more appealing for covering

> ▷ The bold colors of the carpet are echoed in cushions and brickwork, but tempered by the restrained whites of upholstery and surrounding walls.

◁ Rugs in contemporary designs can be enough to soften and warm the harder edges of a home.

armchairs, sofas and ottomans than cottons and linen. Cashmere, alpaca, mohair and fake furs for cushions, bed blankets and throws are even more alluring – small caresses of indulgence that stand out against many of the semi-industrial and sleek materials common to contemporary design. Something as simple as a cashmere throw, in a glowing color such as lilac, placed over the back of a sofa can lift a room.

Sensuality is important, but practicality is just as important a consideration in selecting fabrics. It is not always easy to find the exact texture and color you are looking for, so take good-sized samples home with you and experiment.

With choices for upholstery, ask to see some examples of furniture covered in the same fabric as the one you are thinking of taking. and don't forget to factor in mundane realities such as stain resistance. The choice of fabric for a feeding chair or playroom lounger is naturally going to be very different than the fabric you might choose for a centerpiece sofa in your main living space.

◁ Geometric patterns and strong colors emphasize individuality and help to tranquillize linear spaces.

Splashes of brighter colors and pattern do have a place, especially in private rooms such as bedrooms, although are best treated judiciously. In open-plan environments where space and light are magnified, color and pattern stand out all the more. Perhaps look to the floor rather than to windows or upholstery for an influx of rich pattern. Rugs, dhurries and kilims over wood, stone or concrete flooring warm and soften a room.

Apart from traditional and ethnic choices, contemporary designs in geometric or abstract patterns are commonplace in lofts and apartments as a means of warming and taming a room. Designers such as Eileen Gray, Lucienne Day, Ray Eames, Verner Panton and Michael Graves have been drawn towards textile and carpet design, approaching the medium with a Modernist or Post-Modernist set of principles. If it does not seem too

suede, velvet, linen

This restaurateur's city home was created by combining two apartments in a period building to form one spacious apartment. The owner decided to gut the apartment and shift from a look bordering on traditional country-house chintz to a contemporary take on urban style.

The new look was partly encouraged by professional associations with leading contemporary architects Rick Mather and David Chipperfield, known for their restaurant interiors as well as prestige projects such as the remodeling of the Neue Museum in Berlin (Chipperfield), the architectural addition to the cemetery island of San Michele in Venice (Chipperfield) and the Stein House in London (Mather), which makes great use of glass and metallics and expresses a debt to the example of Modernists such as Le Corbusier and Mies van der Rohe. Such work inspired a modern treatment in this apartment, although scope was somewhat limited by structural constraints.

Joining the two apartments together created a U-shaped space, with a shining steel kitchen – complete with a professional cooking range and black granite floor – created along the old join. All the main rooms were painted in shades of white to bring the apartment together and form a subtle background for the tones and textural qualities of the contemporary furnishings. In the dining room a dining table in American wenge (a dark hardwood) is complemented by gray faux suede dining chairs designed by David Chipperfield, with the texture picked up in the suede chaise longue.

Other modern elements, such as the built-in shelving, mix and contrast with period touches like the fireplace and the

△ **Pattern and color are explored with the curtains, balanced by the earthy and neutral tones elsewhere.**

△ **Steel dominates in the galley-style kitchen, complete with a heavy-duty range stove. Light flows in unimpeded from the bare window.**

◁ **Long modular sofas in cream and the earthy suede of the ottoman create a sense of luxury, with black-and-white photographs prominent against the calm wall colors.**

△ Suede softens metal – the smoothness of the bedside chair sits in contrast to the bed and bedside table.

◁ The ironwork bed is the dramatic focus of this bedroom. The "crown" gives the option for a fabric canopy.

◁ Bright flowers bring vibrancy to the bedroom. Large banks of windows maximize light, which enhances the subtlety of textures and colors.

mirror above it. The curtains in red and green stand out all the more against the neutrality of the rest of the room.

In the living room there is a similar emphasis on neutral and earthy tones. Here, the cream shades of the modular sofa are echoed in the white linen curtains, which are edged in brown velvet. The brown suedes of the large ottoman and the second sofa are echoed in the dark wood surface of the coffee table. The look of the room is all the more effective for being so firmly concentrated on a small range of colors while the strong textural elements soften the space very successfully.

The walls form hanging space for a collection of black-and-white photography, including images by Norman Parkinson and Helmut Newton. The shade of green for the carpet used through all the rooms, except in functional spaces like the kitchen and bathrooms, was specifically chosen and then made to order by a contract manufacturer.

In the main bedroom the emphasis is on maximizing light, and the windows – including a set of French windows that open onto a small balcony – are shrouded only by translucent blinds set close into the frames. In the subdued, clean style of the room a vase of purple flowers stands out as a flash of vibrant color. The en-suite bathroom uses white glass tiles with a soft, glossy porcelain effect to them, with floors in a lightly patterned white marble. Keeping the window bare and painting the ceiling and woodwork white creates a shimmering clean room, with a feel edging towards Minimalism.

The guest bathroom, off a hallway that leads to the other bedrooms in the apartment, takes a different tack, with a bold, neoclassical-style wallpaper and granite floors and surrounds. In a second bedroom an elaborate ironwork bed forms a dramatic centerpoint while banks of built-in cupboards help create a clear and focused environment.

medieval a practice, hanging rugs against the wall like artwork can be an even more dramatic approach than keeping them confined to the floor.

detailing

Within early loft style, architectural elements were raw and basic, with little in the way of finer detailing. But as the influence of loft living has rippled outwards and affected the way in which we approach other urban spaces, the business of detail has become more of a discussion point.

In period apartments and houses it is common to find fireplaces, cornicing, dados, ceiling molds and many other features. We are taught to respect and value such elements and many home owners spend time and effort restoring, reclaiming or carefully replacing them.

When remodeling period homes to bring them in line with a more open, contemporary aesthetic, whether or not to keep hold of these details can present a dilemma. Often, pragmatism leads us in a certain direction. If, when we knock two rooms together the cornicing comes down, too, then it

may make sense to get rid of the cornicing everywhere in the home. The same goes for dados. Cornicing and dados are both features that emphasize the horizontal line of a room and can make the ceiling look lower, which is another reason to lose them. Ceiling moldings may have to go in favor of recessed lighting, doors removed altogether or replaced with glass or translucent partitions. Before long the fireplace may be all that is left.

△ **Artwork and photographs transform this hallway into a personal gallery as well as a thoroughfare.**

▷ **The character of lamps, ceramics and elegantly upholstered furniture makes the difference between a blank space and a home.**

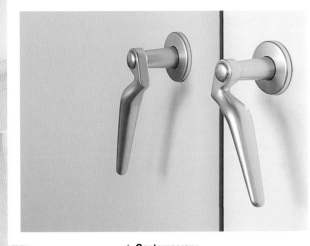

△ **Contemporary details, such as door handles, have now moved away from the ornate towards a sculptural simplicity.**

▷ **A simple combination of contrasting shapes and materials creates a cohesive relaxation zone.**

◁ **A classic Marcel Breuer chair stands out in a contemporary home, enriched by candlelight.**

While there is a need to abide by planning restrictions and building regulations, the truth is that many of these architectural details do belong to a different age. Trying to make them work within a modern, open context that has a different set of priorities, and a different attitude to materials, can therefore be very difficult. Even an ornate fire surround might be best replaced with something simpler in sandstone or chrome.

Compromises can sometimes work. It just depends on how far you want to go, the look you want to achieve. For some, taking away too many reminders of a building's past simply undermines its character. For others, however, period features are impractical, and a real hindrance. Occasional juxtapositions with period fireplaces and other contrasting details, whether period or not – such as a carved Moroccan door or an internal window made with Indian lattice work – can be effective, yet run the risk of becoming the main focus of an entire space.

Contemporary detailing tends towards simplicity and away from the ornate. Door handles, for example, are simply done in steel or ceramic, often

with a sculptural twist. The same could be said of faucets or radiators. Baseboards come in steel or unbeveled wood. Balconies are in steel and glass. The god of good design is still in the detail, but urban style looks firmly towards cohesion and smooth lines.

technology

There has long seemed to be an element of incongruity in the fact that while technology has helped transform the home and make our lives easier and more comfortable, it has also filled up our living spaces with choking machinery and endless clutter: televisions, heating systems, stereos, telephones, computers, ventilation systems, dishwashers, microwaves, laundry machines, refrigerators and more.

Each machine has eaten into our space, taken another set of wires across our territory. Le Corbusier called the home a machine for living, but it is only now that we have managed to develop ways whereby we can hide away the workings of the machine from view.

Heating and ventilation can now be almost invisible. Trench radiators sunken into the floor or underfloor heating remove the necessity for heavy, inescapable, intrusive models while heat and sound insulation cocoon the home more profoundly than ever.

Appliances are shrinking down and the new breeds have become all but silent. Telephones are wireless, so are stereo speakers. Sound systems can be built right into the fabric of the home.

The riot of wires is gradually slipping away. Televisions are all going flat screen, taking up less and less room, and computers are portable and compact.

It seems we are finally reaching a point where the technology of the home is truly unobtrusive, allowing for a better focus on the architecture and interior design of our living space. No doubt there are countless changes and innovations to come that will change the way we live all the more. Yet with proper management they should no longer intrude on valuable home space.

▷ **Arne Jacobsen chairs sit perfectly against a built-in, steel-topped breakfast bar.**

▽ **A chrome spring radiator draws the eye in this bathroom with its abstract, artistic charm.**

utside in

There is an element of lottery about green space in the city. Sometimes green zones — a garden, a terrace, even an extended balcony — come with the territory. But some urban spaces are essentially landlocked, with no opportunity for creating any outside areas to the home. Compromises are often made in choosing an apartment or a house and one of the most common of concessions is doing without a garden. So there is a quality of luxury, of privilege, in outside areas and a feeling that they should be maximized.

▷ **Large windows close to gardens or trees help bring nature into the home, as with this landing, planned in sympathy with a nearby tree.**

Outside living space in the city should be treated inclusively, not exclusively. Gardens or decks are part of the home, part of the total space, and these green rooms offer many possibilities for rest and recreation. Contemporary design tends to treat such areas as an integral part of the home, looking to dissolve barriers between inside and out, with the aim of creating a harmonious connection between the two. The garden becomes the lung of the house, a connection to nature and the seasons, even within the hard and artificial context of the city. It is this very context that makes green space all the more important, as it provides another aspect of sanctuary and retreat within the home environment.

The effects of providing some sort of connection to the outside are partly psychological. Even a view across a park or a communal green zone can be enough to raise the spirits, to give some emotional connection with the natural environment and remind us that there is more to the world than street life and work.

For families, especially, the protected surroundings of a garden or terrace offer children an important, healthy place for play and pleasure.

Within the home there are also opportunities to bring the outside in. One of the benefits of maximizing light and space – of enlarging windows and using glass in architectural fashion – is that it provides a semi-glasshouse atmosphere that encourages plant growth, and is good for the home owners themselves. House plants and flowers will flourish all the more in these conditions, giving owners the opportunity to invent miniature indoor gardens and green spaces.

inside

There are many ways to bring the outside in and erode divisions between the home and its green, outside spaces. The use of glass walls is perhaps the most common way of not only allowing added light into an apartment or house, but of creating a fluid junction with terraces or gardens. In period conversions outside space tends to be at the back of the home, where it is usually more secluded and private. It is here that banks of glass and French windows can be used without too much concern for privacy.

◁ **Walls of glass and decking around this house blur the line between garden and living room.**

Introducing sliding glass doors or French windows can be enough to create that connection between outside and in, to provide an environment akin to that of a glasshouse, where plants and flowers can thrive. Glass walls take the process a step further while many extensions to the backs of houses or ground-floor apartments now make the most of glass structures that go way beyond the scope of traditional conservatories.

It has taken us a surprising amount of time to shrug off our fondness for ornate pavilion structures in the design of conservatories and glasshouses. Even now it is usually better to approach a suitable architect to create a contemporary addition to the home in glass rather than to go to a conservatory supplier. There is now, at least and at last, a wholesale acceptance that glasshouses of any kind should be an intrinsic part of the home and an all-year-round space, at least within the city context, where space is always so valuable.

With improvements in heating and insulation, it is more than possible to create a glasshouse in keeping with a contemporary aesthetic, and which is as friendly, warm and comfortable as any other area in the house. At their best these ultra-modern conservatory rooms can be quite beautiful in themselves, and create a focus for a home. They can work well not just for ground-floor areas, but also for large roof terraces that might benefit from a new, green room.

These are rooms that should be fully integrated into the rest of your living space. They provide dining areas or kitchens, relaxation areas or study zones. They may well form one of the most enticing areas of a home, especially in summer months, so should be exploited to the full.

With new-build, of course, there is an even greater freedom to experiment with fluid intersections. Philip Johnson's Connecticut Glass House or Mies van der Rohe's Farnsworth House provide dynamic examples of demi-glass structures where the surrounding landscape appears to flow through the house itself and become a part of it. These are examples that still stand up very well for contemporary architects.

Extra care must be taken with heating and lighting in glass rooms, and you must make sure the space does not become an oven in summer – perhaps by using blinds or photosensitive glass to control temperatures. Yet glass rooms are natural choices for internal gardens, for sinking bamboo or ficus trees right into the floor – with roots and soil enclosed in recessed metal tubs – for breaking down those traditional barriers between garden and home.

This kind of internal planting takes approaches to treatment of house plants well beyond the occasional rubber tree plant in a terracotta pot to an approach where planting and greenery are considered within the actual design of a space.

Some argue that plants in the home improve the internal atmosphere, are health giving. This may be something of an exaggeration, but what cannot be denied is that introducing greenery into the home in a controlled, considered way promotes a general feeling of wellbeing and acts as a stimulus to forget about the trials of everyday city life.

▷ **A garden terrace, rich with container planting, is a natural extension to this room.**

△ **Large expanses of windows between inside and out emphasize the availability of outside spaces.**

▷ **Decking and
container planting
have been used
to make this roof
terrace into an
outdoor room.
Wooden garden
furniture makes it
a great place for
outdoor eating.**

◁ **This roof terrace is used as a more straight-forward and functional outdoor space, for sunbathing and entertaining.**

terraces

The Manhattan loft was and is mostly self-contained, offering few options for outside living. The same is true of many loft developments around the world, constructed within the carcasses of old, light industrial buildings. One of the few areas that offers an opportunity for a garden or deck is the roof. Go to the top of the Empire State Building or the World Trade Center and look down over the rooftops of New York. You see not only water towers and the hard end of ventilation systems but roof gardens dotted all around Manhattan. Some are democratically divided up into plots to give everyone in the building a slice of outdoor living, some are created as common spaces and others are the preserve of one privileged penthouse owner. And the same is increasingly true of London, Paris and many other progressive urban areas where the hunt for outside space has sent people upwards.

Roof gardens can compete well with traditional gardens in terms of variety and richness. There are restrictions on a roof garden to do with

weight, dampness and root damage, as well as basic safety concerns such as suitable perimeters and protective balconies, but it is not that unusual to find lawns, shrubbery and borders – and container gardening of all kinds – going on high above the city streets.

Planning a roof terrace depends on what it will actually be used for and the lifestyle of its owners. For some, creating and maintaining an elaborate, complex garden with a wealth of planting and greenery will be one of life's most pleasurable pursuits. Others will prefer a more functional, low-maintenance space for play and entertaining, for barbecues and distractions, and may opt for a simple deck treatment with container planting to soften the look. Whatever your approach, roof terraces can offer a superior haven when you crave a fresh-air boost.

Basic structural elements on a roof terrace, such as a water tower or chimney stack, can limit the design. Often, the best way around this is not to pretend these elements don't exist, but to make a feature of them. Plant around them with climbers and

an indoor oasis

A total reinvention of this period home by a former academic turned environmental designer has created a calm, contemporary space which emphasizes connections between outside and in. A new steel caged frame allowed for the removal or repositioning of many internal walls and floors.

The most dramatic element of this space is a double-height dining area, made by removing a section of the ground-floor level to create a large atrium that stretches upwards from the basement. Within this atrium a natural theme has been established with towering bamboo trees planted right into recessed containers in the floor. A connection between outside and in has also been established by a small river that flows through channels in the floor and appears to intersect with a waterfall in the front garden. Slatted maple bridges protect the channels, with gaps where you can see and hear the water trickling through over small slabs of black slate.

The effect, partly influenced by the work of Japanese designers and architects such as Tadao Ando, is extraordinary. The use of very modern materials – such as poured concrete for the floors, with a pure white pigment ground into the mix, and glass and steel for the balustrade that borders the atrium at ground-floor level – sits well in juxtaposition with these natural elements. The restraint in the use of color, with the earth tones of the artwork, or the warm shades of wooden furniture set against the white walls, allows the drama of the internal architecture to shine through.

The dining area connects directly into the kitchen, which in turn connects to the back garden, so creating an uninter-rupted flow of light from front to back and a common currency in the natural theme. While the front garden is dominated by the waterfall, which is all the more visually alluring when illuminated at night, the rear garden forms a more functional space, providing an outside dining and entertaining area complete with wooden table and benches, and a built-in outdoor heater to allow for all-year use.

◁ **Bamboo and palms lend a greenhouse feel to the dining room atrium, complete with flowing river.**

△ **Palms and window boxes reinforce the outside in theme.**

◁ **Bamboo trees encased in water-proof, concrete planters have been recessed into the floor for an indoor garden.**

▽ **The waterfall in the front garden is illuminated at night with lights sunken into the tiered pools.**

◁ Dramatic, high-reaching palms give the space a tropical feel.

▷ An outdoor heater positioned in the back garden – adjoining the kitchen – makes this a space for all-year-round eating and entertaining.

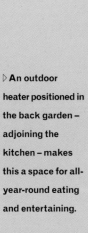

◁ The dining room runs directly into the kitchen and back garden, taking the natural theme straight through from the front to the back of the house.

Upstairs, on the first floor, a small orchid garden has been created to one side over a floor panel of frosted glass, allowing extra light to filter up through the plants from the atrium below. The orchid garden is complemented by windows and French doors – which open onto a small balcony – to each side of the space. Here, again, light filters through from one side of the house to the other while at night recessed ceiling lights are complemented by the glow of light filtering up from the frosted-glass panel.

On the top floor of the house, which has a study area, the owner wished to create a roof terrace but was refused planning permission. His solution was to invent an electric retracting roof that provides a similar atmosphere to a terrace, while palm trees in containers add a green element.

The whole house manages to pull off the difficult trick of creating a sympathetic marriage between contemporary urban style and an emphasis on the natural world and outside space. In the bathroom, for instance, there is a concrete tub with an integrated heating filament – representing the most sophisticated of aesthetic choices – yet the bathroom still retains a very natural feeling in color and texture, with terracotta bowls, and earthy browns for the walls and wooden floors.

It is a home where the priorities of open living and maximized light are to the fore, yet where there is also a strong emphasis on texture, contrast, and comfort. The home represents a fine example of green living and offers the best of everything within the contemporary urban space.

creepers, paint them, or use spot-lighting to make them into a centerpoint.

Even the smallest roof terrace or balcony area can offer some reassuring connection with the outside world. French doors can be thrown open on a sunny day, and container gardening adds touches of life. Perhaps you are lucky enough to have room to sit out and eat. Even the most basic elements of outside space can be rewarding and enticing if treated in a responsive and considered manner.

gardens

City gardens should be created in sympathy with the interior design of the home. The transition from inside to out should be a natural one, rather than a jolt, with an approach to materials that fits in with the overall aesthetic. A transitional area between outdoors and in can be an effective design statement in itself. It may be that a glass room forms that area, but alternatives might be a verandah, canopy or deck that blurs the line between home and garden. These are solutions that help make the garden appear easily available and accessible,

△ **Courtyards, verandahs and colonnades help diffuse the barrier between indoors and out.**

◁ **Changes in materials and surfacing help divide and zone larger garden spaces and outdoor rooms.**

a reminder that garden space is there to be used and not neglected. At the same time, decks or verandahs can create a delineated zone for eating and entertaining, as well as offering shade on too hot a day.

In larger gardens the idea of zoning can help in the design. Different parts of the garden can be subtly divided up into areas for eating and outdoor cooking, for relaxing, for children's play and as areas for borders and gardening itself. In smaller gardens it becomes more important to prioritize the use to which the garden is going to be put and then plan accordingly.

Many city gardens tend to be overshadowed to some extent by surrounding buildings, so consider what can be done to maximize light in the garden and through the garden into the house. If trees and plants have become overgrown and are constricting the space, then take action to lop and cut back the vegetation or perhaps look at a more ambitious scheme that allows replanting. Consult a garden designer or tree surgeon if you have difficulty seeing beyond the creeping jungle outside the door.

Use light materials such as sandstone, bright-toned slate or other kinds of paving slabs. Don't worry about weathering, as weathered stone or brick simply adds more character to outside spaces. Adding areas of ceramic tile or mosaic within the stone helps break up large areas, assists in zoning and allows splashes of color. Alternatively, look at the simplicity of light gravels, pebbles or even sand – taking inspiration from the elegant restraint and serenity of Japanese gravel gardens – that can be raked into sculptural patterns. Mirrors or reflective metal panels fixed to garden walls can help reflect light and create the illusion of increased dimensions.

Garden furniture, planters and containers can complement interior style. As well as wood, consider alternatives in metal and plastics that have more of a flavor of modernity. Contemporary ceramic planters glazed in bold colors add bolts of color as well as textural contrast. Color can raise a garden above the ordinary, as in the famous Jardin Majorelle in Marrakesh. Here, the rich indigo colors used for walkways, the surrounds of water pools, planters and buildings create a sumptuous effect and a startling backdrop to the bamboo, dwarf palms, bougainvillea and nasturtiums.

Think of the garden as one of the most sensual spaces of the home and plant herbs and flowers with strong scents: jasmine, lavender, lilac or honeysuckle. Water features are soothing to eye and ear, and water can be treated in a very contemporary fashion, using pools, water spouts and linear water courses combined with metals or ceramics for watertight surfaces and exposed conduits. Fish pools and water planting (water lilies,

▷ **Even small gardens and green walkways can be treated as semi-integrated parts of the home, with container gardening and climbing creepers.**

▽ **Greenery and planting helps to soften the fabric of the home, both outside and in.**

duckweed and reeds) can be more complex, yet add to the many layers of interest within the garden. Just be careful to adequately protect exposed areas of water if toddlers or young children are using the space.

The tendency in planting urban gardens is towards the use of the more sculptural plants that create blocks of contrasting shapes: feathery papyrus, palm fronds and agave, hummocks of miscanthus grass, ribbed hostas and the pom pom shapes of *Allium giganteum*. Creating an order and a pattern helps simplify and accentuate the semi-architectural effect of the plants themselves – a garden may be successfully designed around one central feature such as a palm or plane tree. Concentrated blocks of planting allow a more vivid show of color and form.

One of the benefits of city gardens is that they tend to be less exposed than country equivalents and so less likely to be damaged by extremes in temperature. Many large Western cities have a micro-climate that is a degree or two higher than that of their surrounding areas, so city-center dwellers may find they can experiment with more exotic planting than would survive elsewhere in the region. In shaded areas extra care is often needed to find plants that will still flourish without strong bursts of exposed sunlight, such as hellebores, hostas, ostrich ferns and violets. Or others that will tolerate partial shade, such as foxgloves, asters and honesty.

Much city planting tends towards low-maintenance greenery with a sculptural quality, but it can be beneficial to try to plant with the passing months in mind, allowing yourself cover and color right through the seasons, seeing the garden as an all-year space. The garden should be, after all, one more valuable room.

resources

LIGHTING

Artemide SpA
Via Bergamo 18
20010 Pregnana Milanese
Milan
Italy
Tel: +39 2 935 181
Tel (in USA): (631) 694 9292
www.artemide.com

Belux AG
Bremgarterstrasse 109
5610 Wohlen
Switzerland
Tel: +41 56 618 73 73
Tel (in USA): (201) 585 9420
www.belux.com

ERCO Leuchten GmbH
Brockhauser Weg 80-82
58505 Lüdenscheid
Germany
Tel: +49 2351 551 0
Tel (in USA): (732) 225 8856
www.erco.com

Estiluz SA
Ctra de Ogassa s/n
17860 Sant Joan de les Abadesses
Girona
Spain
Tel: +34 72 72 01 25
Tel (in USA): (201) 641 1997
www.arrakis.es/~estiluz

Flos SpA
Via Angelo Faini 2
25073 Bovezzo
Italy
Tel: +39 030 24381
Tel (in USA): (631) 549 2746
www.flos.net

Leucos Srl
Via Treviso 77
30037 Scorze
Venice
Italy
Tel: +39 041 585 9111
Tel (in USA): (732) 225 0010
www.leucos.com

Luceplan SpA
Via E. T. Moneta 46
20161 Milan
Italy
Tel: +39 02 662 421
Tel (in USA): (212) 989 6265
www.luceplan.com

Luxo ASA
PO Box 60 Manglerod
Enebakkvn 117
0612 Oslo
Norway
Tel: +47 22 57 40 00
Tel (in USA): (914) 937 4433
www.luxo.com

**FURNITURE
& FURNISHINGS**

Arc Linea Arredanebti SpA
Viale Pasubio 50
36030 Caldogno
Italy
Tel: +39 0444 394111
www.arclinea.it

Cappellini SpA
Via Marconi 35
22060 Arosio
Italy
Tel: +39 031 759 111
Tel (in USA): (212) 966 0669
www.cappellini.it

Cattelan Arrendamenti
Via Manzoni 6
36010 Zanè
Italy
Tel: +39 445 362815
www.cattelan.it

The Conran Shop
Michelin House
81 Fulham Road
London SW3 6RD
England
Tel: +44 020 7589 7401
Tel (in USA): (212) 755 9079
www.conran.com

Crucial Trading Ltd
PO Box 11
Duke Place
Kidderminster
Worcestershire DY10 2JR
England
Tel: +44 1562 825 0
www.crucial-trading.com

Muurame
PST-Moduli Oy
Pikitie 2
15560 Nastola
Finland
Tel: +358 3 7801241
muurame.com

Neotu
25, rue du Renard
75004 Paris
France
Tel: +33 1 42 78 96 97
Tel (in USA): (212) 695 9404
www.neotu.com

Quattrocchio Srl
Via Isonzo 51
15100 Alessandria
Italy
Tel: +39 0131 445 361
Tel (in USA): (401) 724 4470
Tel (in USA): (212) 925 3615
www.tinteunite.it/italiandesign/quat
trocchio/default.html

Rosenthal Einrichtung
Hindenburgring 9
32339 Espetkamp
Germany
Tel: +49 5772 2090
Tel (in USA): (201) 804 8000
www.rosenthal.de

Sellex SA
Donosti Ibildea 84
Poligono 26
20115 Astigarraga-Ergobia
Guipuzcoa
Spain
Tel: +34 943 557 011
www.sidi.es/sellex

Tre-P SpA
Via dell'Industria 2
20034 Birone di Giussano
Italy
Tel: +39 0362 861120
www.trep-trepiu.com

Vitra
Klünenfeldstrasse 22
4127 Birsfelden
Switzerland
Tel: +41 061 377 0000
Tel (in USA): (212) 539 1900
www.vitra.com

STONE & CERAMICS

The Amtico Company
Kingfield Road
Coventry CV6 5AA
England
Tel: +44 024 7686 1400
Tel (in USA): (404) 267 1900
www.amtico.com

Attica
543 Battersea Park Road
London SW11 3BL
England
Tel: +44 020 7738 1234
www.attica.co.uk

Euromarble
155 Bowes Road
New Southgate
London N11 2JA
England
Tel: +44 020 8888 2304
www.euromarble.co.uk

Fired Earth (Tiling & Flooring)
Twyford Mill
Oxford Road
Adderbury
Oxfordshire OX17 3HP
England
Tel: +44 1295 814315
www.firedearth.co.uk

Gruppo Ceramiche Ricchetti
Via Radici in Piano 428
41049 Sassuolo
Italy
Tel: +44 0536 865111
Tel (in USA): (407) 984 0505
www.ricchetti.it

Kirkstone Quarries Ltd
Skelwith Bridge
Ambleside
Cumbria LA22 9NN
England
Tel: +44 015394 33296
www.kirkstone.com

Mosaic Workshop
443-449 Holloway Road
London N7 6LJ
England
Tel: +44 020 7263 2997
www.mosaicworkshop.com

Paris Ceramics
583 Kings Road
London SW6 2EH
England
Tel: +44 020 7371 7778
Tel (in USA): (212) 644 2782
Tel (in USA): (203) 862 9538
Tel (in USA): (312) 467 9830
Tel (in USA): (323) 658 8570
Tel (in USA): (561) 835 8875
Tel (in USA): (415) 490 5430
Tel (in USA): (617) 261 9736
www.parisceramics.com

Porcelanosa Grupo
Carretera N-340
PO Box 131
12540 Villarreal
Castellón
Spain
Tel: +34 964 507 1001
Tel (in USA): (631) 845 7070
www.porcelanosa.com

Terra Firma Tiles
70 Chalk Farm Road
London NW1 8AN
England
Tel: +44 020 7485 7227
www.terrafirmatiles.co.uk

Rover Stone Color & Design SrL
Strada della Giara 23
37030 Poiano
Italy
Tel: +39 045 526 322
Tel (in USA): 800 362 7191
www.roverstone.com

GLASS

Blu
The Barn
Pilmore Lane
Watchfield
Somerset TA9 4LB
England
Tel: +44 01278 79 36 44
www.blu-uk.com

F A Firman (specialist builders)
19 Bates Road
Harold Wood
Romford
Essex RM3 0JH
England
Tel: +44 01708 374534
www.f-a-firman.demon.co.uk

Langley London (glass bricks)
Harling House
47-51 Great Suffolk Street
London SE1 0SR
England
Tel: +44 020 7803 4444
www.langleyuk.co.uk

Foscarini Murano SpA
Via delle Industrie 92
30020 Marcon
Italy
Tel: +39 041 595 1199
www.foscarini.com

AV Mazzega SrL
Via Vivarini 3
30141 Murano
Italy
Tel: +39 041 736 677
www.avmazzega.com

Ozone Glass Design Pty Ltd
144 Old Pittwater Road
Brookvale NSW 2100
Australia
Tel: +61 2 9938 5088
www.ozoneglass.com.au

Pilkington plc
Prescot Road
St Helens
Merseyside WA10 3TT
England
Tel: +44 01744 28882
Tel (in Canada): (416) 421 9000
www.pilkington.com

Pittsburgh Corning Corp
800 Presque Isle Drive
Pittsburgh, Pennsylvania 15239
USA
Tel: (724) 327 6100
www.pittsburghcorning.com

Solarglass Ltd
Herald Way
Binley
Coventry CV3 2ND
England
Tel: +44 01203 458844
www.solarglass.co.uk

Stained Glass Assoc of America
4450 Fenton Road
Hartland, Michigan 48353
USA
Tel: (800) 888 7422
www.stainedglass.org

STEEL

D-Line Intl AS
Carl Jacobsens Vej 28
1790 Copenhagen V
Denmark
Tel: +45 36 180400
www.dline.com

Dierre
Strada Statale per Chieri
Villanova d'Asti
Italy
Tel: +39 0141 94 94 11
www.dierre-spa.it

HEWI
Heinrich Wilke GmbH
Prof. Bierstrasse 1-5
34454 Bad Arolsen
Germany
Tel: +49 056 91 820
Tel (in USA): (717) 293 1313
www.hewi.com

Nusteel Ltd
Lympne Industrial Estate
Lympne
Hythe
Kent CT21 4LR
England
Tel: +44 01303 268112
www.nusteel.demon.co.uk

WOODS

The Hardwood Flooring Company
146-152 West End Lane
London NW6 1SD
England
Tel: +44 020 7328 8481
www.hardwood-flooring.uk.com

Hartco
PO Box 4009
Oneida, Tennesee 37841
USA
Tel: (800) 769 8528
www.hartcoflooring.com

Junckers Industrier AS
Vaertsvej
4600 Køge
Denmark
Tel: +45 56 65 18 95
Tel (in USA) (714) 777 6430
www.junckershardwood.com

Kentucky Wood Floors Inc
PO Box 33276
Louisville, Kentucky 40232
USA
Tel: (502) 451 6024
www.kentuckywood.com

National Hardwood Lumber Assoc
PO Box 34518
Memphis, Tennessee 38184
USA
Tel: (901) 377 1818
www.natlhardwood.org

Rowi Parket International BV
Rowi Productie BV
Kruiskamp 3
6071 KM Swalmen
The Netherlands
Tel: +31 475 501 520
www.rowi.nl

Walcot Reclamation
108 Walcot Street
Bath
Avon BA1 5BG
England
Tel: +44 01225 444404
www.walcot.com

Wicanders / Amorim (UK) Ltd
Amorim House
Star Road, Partridge Green
nr Horsham, West Sussex
England RH13 8RA
Tel: +44 01403 710002
www.wicanders.com

DETAILS

ABC Carpet & Home (accessories)
888 Broadway
New York, New York 10003
USA
Tel: (212) 473 3000
www.abchome.com

Albini & Fontanot SpA (stairs)
Via P. Paolo Pasolini 6
47852 Cerasolo Ausa
Italy
Tel: +39 0541 906111
www.albiniefontanot.com

Alessi SpA (accessories)
Via Privata Alessi 6
28882 Crusinallo, Italy
Tel: +44 0323 86 86 11
Tel (in USA): (212) 431 1310
www.alessi.it

Allgood (handles, fittings etc)
297 Euston Road
London NW1 3AQ
England
Tel: +44 020 7387 9951
www.allgood.co.uk

Bisque Radiators
15 Kingsmead Square
Bath
Avon BA1 2AE, England
Tel: +44 01225 469244
www.leonardouk.com/bisque

Levolor Home Fashions (shades)
4110 Premier Drive
High Point, North Carolina 27265
USA
Tel: (800) 232 2028
www.levolor.com

Simpson Door Co
400 Simpson Avenue
McCleary, Washington 98557
USA
Tel: (360) 495 3291
www.simpson.com

V'Soske Joyce Ltd (rugs)
Oughterard
Co. Galway
Ireland
Tel: +353 91 82113
www.failte.com/vsoske

SURFACES

Avonite Inc
1945 Highway 304
Belen, New Mexico 87002
USA
Tel: (505) 864 3800
www.avonite.com

Abet Laminati SpA
Viale Industria 21
12042 Bra
Italy
Tel: +44 0172 419 111
Tel (in USA): (201) 541 0700
www.abet-laminati.it

Forbo Nairn Ltd
PO Box 1
Den Road
Kikcaldy
Fife KY1 2SB
Scotland
Tel: +44 1592 643 111
www.forbo.com

Tarkett Sommer AG
Nachtweideweg 1-7
67227 Frankenthal
Germany
Tel: +49 6233 81 0
Tel (in USA): (423) 928 3122
Tel (in USA): (610) 266 5500
www.tarkett-sommer.com

BATHROOMS

Aloys F. Dornbracht GmbH & Co KG
Armaturenfabrik
Köbbingser Mühle 6
58640 Iserlohn
Germany
Tel: +49 2371 4330
Tel (in USA): (800) 774 1181
www.dornbracht.com

Alternative Plans
9 Hester Road
London SW11 4AN
England
Tel: +44 020 7228 6460
www.alternative-plans.co.uk

Avante Bathroom Products
Dragon Court
Springwell Road
Leeds LS12 1EY
England
Tel: +44 0113 244 5337
www.avante-bathroom-products.co.uk

Colourwash
63-65 Fulham High Street
London SW6 3JJ
England
Tel: +44 020 7371 0911
www.colourwash.co.uk

Czech & Speake
39c Jermyn Street
London SW1Y 6DN
England
Tel: +44 020 7439 0216
www.czechspeake.com

Hastings Tile & Bath
30 Commercial Street
Freeport, New York 11520
USA
Tel: (516) 379 3500
www.hastingstilebath.com

Ideal-Standard Ltd
Boulevard du Soverain 348
1160 Brussels
Belgium
Tel: +32 2 678 0911
www.ideal-standard.com

Kartell SpA
Via Turati Angolo
Carlo Porta 1
20121 Milan
Italy
Tel: +39 02 659 7916
www.kartell.it

Kroin Inc
180 Fawcett Street
Cambridge, Massachusetts 02138
USA
Tel: (617) 492 4000
www.kroin.com

Ponsi Rubinetterie Toscane
Via A. Volta 2
55049 Viareggio
Italy
Tel: +39 0584 427611
www.ponsi.it

Svedbergs i Dalstorp AB
Verkstadsvägen 1
51463 Dalstorp
Sweden
Tel: +46 321 26500
www.svedbergs.se

West One Bathrooms
130-138 Garratt Lane
London SW18 4EE
England
Tel: +44 020 8870 2121
www.westonebathrooms.com

KITCHENS

Robert Bosch GmbH
Robert Bosch Platz 1
Gerlingenschillerhoele
70839 Stuttgart
Germany
Tel: +49 711 811 0
Tel (in USA): (708) 865 5200
www.boschappliances.com

Bulthaup GmbH & Co
84153 Aich
Germany
Tel: +49 1802 212534
Tel (in USA): (310) 288 3875
www.bulthaup.com

Dacor
950 South Raymond Avenue
Pasadena, California 91109
USA
Tel: (626) 799 1000
www.dacorappl.com

Franke AG
Dorfbachstrasse
4663 Aaarburg
Switzerland
Tel: +41 62 787 3431
Tel (in USA): (215) 822 6590
www.franke.com

Friedrich Grohe AG
Haupstrasse 137
58675 Hemer
Germany
Tel: +49 2372 930
Tel (in USA): (630) 582 7711
www.grohe.com

Miele & Cie GmbH
Carl Miele Strasse 29
33332 Güetersloh
Germany
Tel: +49 5421 890
Tel (in USA): (609) 419 9898
www.mieleusa.com

Poggenpohl GmbH & Co
Herringhauser Strasse 33
32051 Herford
Germany
Tel: +49 5221 3810
Tel (in USA): (973) 812 8900
www.poggenpohl.de

Smeg SpA
Via Circonvallazione Nord 36
42016 Guastalla
Italy
Tel: +39 0522 83 77 77
www.smeg.it

index